EMPIRES OF MYSTERY

THE INCAS, THE ANDES, AND LOST CIVILIZATIONS

EMPIRES OF MYSTERY

THE INCAS, THE ANDES, AND LOST CIVILIZATIONS

Text by
Federico Kauffman-Doig

•

Translated by
Eulogio Guzmán

Presented by

florida
International museum

Organized by
WONDERS: The Memphis International Cultural Series
in association with PromPerú and the Instituto Nacional de Cultura del Perú

Published by Lithograph Publishing Company,
a division of Lithograph Printing Company,
a division of Master Graphics

Printed in the United States of America
Library of Congress Catalog Card Number: 98-060503
ISBN 1-882516-09-5 (hardcover)
ISBN 1-882516-08-7 (paperback)
Second Printing

Project Manager: Russ Gordon
Catalogue Production: Garrett White, Los Angeles
Editor: Garrett White
Graphic Design: Neville Burtis, Mackie Osborne, Garrett White
Editorial Staff: Karen Hansgen, Wendy Sand
Photographer: Philipp Scholz Rittermann

Production Coordinator: Gloria Morarity, Connie Reeves
Color Separations and Printing:
Lithograph Printing Company

Cover design: Yessawich, Pepperdine and Brown
Object photograph: Philipp Scholz Rittermann, Gold Tumi, Sicán, A.D. 700–1370.
Back cover: Wolfgang Kaehler, Doorway, Machu Picchu, Inca, A.D. 1200–1532.

Contents

Letter from the Mayor of St. Petersburg

In January 1995, the Florida International Museum opened its doors to Russian culture with the outstanding inaugural exhibit, *Treasures of the Czars*. The museum has since led thousands of visitors through the lands of Egypt and Greece, and to the watery depths of the North Atlantic. Now, residents and visitors will travel to Peru with the opening on October 23, 1998, of *Empires of Mystery: The Incas, the Andes, and Lost Civilizations.*

The largest exhibition of Peruvian artifacts ever in the United States, the more than 300 artifacts span several thousand years of the history of some of the most complex and sophisticated civilizations ever known in the Western Hemisphere. As with previous shows, *Empires of Mystery* offers a wonderful educational opportunity for school children, who will enjoy curriculum support in the classroom combined with visits to the museum.

Coming off of the incredible success represented by more than 830,000 visitors to *TITANIC: The Exhibition*, the Florida International Museum is enjoying local, national, and international attention for the quality, uniqueness, and educational value of its exhibits. As a result, the museum has become a linchpin in the success and rebuilding of St. Petersburg's downtown, joining in a beneficial partnership with other museums, merchants, restaurants, The Pier, and our community as a whole.

Without the generous support of our business sponsors and organizations and individuals from the community, a project such as *Empires of Mystery* would not be possible. I would like to thank the St. Petersburg City Council and the Florida International Museum Board of Directors for bringing this next exhibition to St. Petersburg.

I would also like to express my gratitude to museum President and C.E.O. Joseph F. Cronin, his staff, and the more than 1,000 volunteers who have contributed countless hours to ensure that this latest show will have a successful and smooth run in our city.

Sincerely,

David J. Fischer
Mayor

Letter from the Ambassador of Peru

Embassy of Peru
Washington, DC 20036

I would like to thank the city of St. Petersburg for having selected the pre-Inca cultures of Peru as the subject of this year's Florida International Museum exhibition. The objects you will see on display and in this catalogue span more than two millennia of Peru's cultural history, and constitute some of the most exquisite vestiges of one of the few endogenous or "pristine" civilizations in the world.

Empires of Mystery: The Incas, the Andes, and Lost Civilizations is the result of three years of cooperation between public and private Peruvian cultural institutions and the city of Memphis, Tennessee, and constitutes one of the most ambitious and aesthetically successful displays on Peru ever organized in the United States. I hope that it will prove to be an enriching experience for all interested in pre-Columbian cultures, and a propitious opportunity for enhancing the knowledge of Peru in the heartland of America.

Moreover, this gathering is a significant instrument for linking two nations that are both truly multiracial and pluricultural. Perhaps in these two facets lie the dynamism and potential necessary for our two countries to confirm the New World's essence as a place for hope and a home for creativity. The Peruvian Embassy is very proud to have cooperated in this endeavor.

Ricardo V. Luna
Ambassador

Letter from the Chairman of the Board

Welcome to *Empires of Mystery: The Incas, the Andes, and Lost Civilizations*.

This remarkable collection of artifacts and the story they tell transport the visitor to the mysteries and intrigue of a culture and a civilization thousands of years old.

This is the fifth exhibition presented by the Florida International Museum. First was *Treasures of the Czars*, a story of the Romanov Dynasty. Next came *Splendors of Ancient Egypt*, the story of four thousand years of ancient pharaohs, followed by *Alexander the Great* and stories from ancient Greece.

TITANIC: The Exhibition commenced Phase II in the life of the Florida International Museum. *Titanic* drew over 830,000 attendees, one of the largest attendances achieved for a cultural exhibition in the history of the United States. More than 100,000 school children attended in organized school groups.

The Florida International Museum is only one of the many cultural and entertainment venues along the waterfront of St. Petersburg. The museums, galleries, theaters, and boutiques found here combine to make St. Petersburg one of the cultural centers of the southeast United States.

On behalf of the directors, staff, and volunteers of the Florida International Museum, we thank you for visiting *Empires of Mystery*.

Very truly yours,

Richard M. Baker
Chairman of the Board
Florida International Museum

Letter from the President and C.E.O.

Today, thanks to a dramatic change in the way the museum is operated and the incredible success of the TITANIC exhibition, the Florida International Museum's future looks bright. While drawing over 830,000 visitors during its six-month run, *TITANIC: The Exhibition* became one of the highest attended exhibits in the history of the United States. This did not come about by chance. It is a result of a renaissance in virtually all aspects of the museum's operations, coupled with aggressive marketing and public relations outreach programs to the media, the hospitality industry, and the public. It is important to remember that this renaissance could not have occurred without the initial financial support of the founding underwriters, John and Rosemary Galbraith, St. Petersburg Times, Florida Progress Corporation, and the City of St. Petersburg.

The past year also marked a major change in the leadership of the Florida International Museum with the retirement of the museum's founding chairman and major benefactor, John William Galbraith, who was elected to the position of Chairman Emeritus. In his place, Richard M. Baker picked up the reins of leadership and helped place the museum on solid financial ground while developing a strategic plan for future exhibitions and the development of the entire complex into a cultural-educational center for the community. I would like to express my special appreciation to W. Richard Johnston for the key role he played in the museum's turnaround through his advice, guidance, and strong support.

Thanks also go to our friends and partners in Memphis, Tennessee, especially to Mr. Glen Campbell, Executive Director of Wonders: The Memphis International Cultural Series, for the outstanding working relationship that has been established with the Florida International Museum. For this magnificent Peruvian exhibition we are greatly indebted to the Instituto Nacional de Cultura del Perú and PromPerú, along with the lending institutions listed in this catalogue.

Lastly, it is to the entire museum staff that I extend my most heartfelt thanks and appreciation. They faced an enormous challenge in the past year to build new programs, systems, and plans to refocus the museum's operation and accommodated unprecedented crowds with enthusiasm and professionalism. Together with our volunteers, who are the heart and soul of this museum, they have molded a team that will allow us to continue to serve you, our visitors, and to play a major role in Florida's cultural and educational history.

Cordially,

Joseph F. Cronin
President & C.E.O.

Letter from PromPerú

Peru Invites You . . .

"Past is prologue," which is what makes *Empires of Mystery: The Incas, the Andes, and Lost Civilizations* so magical. The colorful Peruvian past on display for you in Memphis served as the introductory stanzas in a concert of creativity that Peru continues to compose today. The grand advances of our ancient grandparents—healing herbs harvested by Amazonian *curanderos*, hydraulics devised by the Moche, Chavín de Huántar architectural principles employed three millennia later in a successful military operation—nourish our *creatividad criolla*, the diehard Peruvian spirit of innovation through which we continuously imbue Peru's ancient traditions with fresh life.

Our ancestors would be proud to see that their multitude of languages and cultures gives Peru a competitive edge in today's multilingual, multicultural marketplace. And we are gratified that with this global market—with international exhibits like this one, for example—Peru is strengthening its most traditional identities.

Two miles high in the Andean sky, the mythical ruins of Sacsahuaman testify that the Incas, too, learned from their ancestors. While assembling the ancient roots of Peru into a powerful state, they fashioned this fortress of boulders cut so exactly that a leaf of paper will not slide into the seam. Now, Peruvians in the mountains outside Lima are employing the Incas' stone cutting techniques in developing the area's thermal baths. They are perfecting the trade and building their own economic future.

It is more than simply mimicking the Incas or their ancestors. Rather than building a replica of our rich past, we are tending it in order to cultivate a future with deep roots. This marvelous exhibit in Memphis offers the opportunity to explore some of those roots. If you are a discoverer by heart, come explore the Peru that has flowered up from the roots we have on display. Thanks to Memphis, it is you who can best testify that our past is part of our future. That is the true magic of *Empires of Mystery: The Incas, the Andes, and Lost Civilizations*.

¡Amigos, bienvenidos al Perú!

Beatriz Boza
President, PromPerú
Peru's Tourism and Investment Promotion Board

Letter from the
Instituto Nacional de Cultura del Perú

Peru and its Historical Continuity

We at the Instituto Nacional de Cultura are excited about our participation in creating the exhibition *Empires of Mystery: The Incas, the Andes, and Lost Civilizations*. This exhibit is made up of 332 cultural goods that are part of the cultural patrimony of the Peruvian nation. Three hundred and seventeen of the pieces were loaned for the exhibit by the Museo Nacional de Arqueología, Antropología e Historía del Perú, which is part of the Sistema Nacional de Museos. The remaining pieces came from private collections. This exhibit is an example of the joint efforts of all of these agencies.

From April 16 through September 16, 1998, this exhibition will be presented at The Pyramid in Memphis, TN. It will then travel to the Florida International Museum in Saint Petersburg, Florida. Those who visit the exhibit will witness Peru's cultural achievements as well as its rich past, which are represented in both the cultural creations and traditions of our ancestors.

According to the layout employed by our experts, *Empires of Mystery: The Incas, the Andes, and Lost Civilizations* offers a complete picture of Peru's ancient civilizations. The exhibit is a grand mural of Peru's history presented with temporal continuity and spatial unity.

As National Director of the Instituto Nacional de Cultura del Perú, I would like to thank everyone who has contributed to the success of this exhibit. I would also like to extend my most cordial greetings to everyone who attends the exhibit, with the hope that the aesthetic contemplation of all of these objects will make them feel closer to my country.

Luis Arista Montoya
National Director
Instituto Nacional de Cultura del Perú

Peru Organizing Committee

Republic of Peru Organizing Committee

Under the Patronage of
His Excellency Alberto Fujimori
President of the Republic of Peru

Executive Committee
His Excellency Domingo Palermo
Minister of Education

His Excellency Ricardo V. Luna
Ambassador of the Republic of Peru to the United States of America

Dr. Beatriz Boza
President of PromPerú

Señor Luis Arista Montoya
National Director of the Instituto Nacional de Cultura

Planning Committee
Rocío Fernández Lores
Executive Secretary of PromPerú

Arquitecta Flor de María Valladolid
Executive Director of the Instituto Nacional de Cultura

Dr. Fernando Rosas
Director of the Museo Nacional de Arqueología, Antropología e Historía del Perú

Señora Rosa Amano
Director of the Fundación Museo Amano

Señor Dionisio Romero
President of the Banco de Crédito del Perú

Lic. Clyde Valladolid
President of the Museo de Sitio de Huallamarca

Dr. Luis Watanabe
Director of the Museo de la Nación

Dr. Federico Kauffmann-Doig
Director of the Instituto de Arqueología Amazonica

Lenders

The Florida International Museum expresses its profound gratitude to the following museums and institutions for the loan of objects for this exhibition:

Museo Nacional de Arqueología, Antropología e Historía del Perú

Fundación Museo Amano

Banco de Crédito del Perú

Banco Weise, Perú

Instituto de Arqueología Amazonica

Museo de Sitio de Huallamarca

Jon Thompson

Enhancing this exhibition has been made possible with the help of United States Customs Service Southeast Region, of the Department of the Treasury and the U.S. Attorney's Office of the Department of Justice, Southern District of Florida.

And the kind permission of the Government of the Republic of Peru, including His Excellency the President of The Republic of Peru Alberto Fujimori

The Ministry of Foreign Affairs, The Office of Cultural Affairs for the Ministry of Foreign Affairs, The Ministry of Education, The Institute of National Culture and Consulate of Peru in Miami.

Underwriters and Major Sponsors

Founding Underwriters
City of St. Petersburg
St. Petersburg Times
Florida Progress Corporation
John and Rosemary Galbraith

Major Sponsors
A.A.A.
Aero Peru
Bayfront–St. Anthony's Health Care, Inc.
Continental Airlines
Creative Solutions Interactive, Inc.
Eller Media Company
Florida Coca-Cola Bottling Company
Fortress FAE^{SM} Worldwide
PAX-66 WXPX-TV
Raymond James
Renaissance Vinoy Resort
SouthTrust Bank N.A. West Florida
St. Petersburg/Clearwater Area Convention
  & Visitors Bureau
St. Petersburg Times
University of South Florida,
  St. Petersburg Campus
WTVT - Fox 13

Sponsors

Apex Advanced Payment Exchange, Inc.
Busch Gardens Tampa Bay
C. J. Publishers, Inc.
Capital One
Catering By Lundy's
Clear Channel Communications
Coast 107.5
Columbia Restaurant
Don CeSar Beach Resort & Spa
Federated Department Stores
Fisher & Sauls, P.A.
Irwin Contracting, Inc.
JMC Communities–Developer of Florencia
Florida Suncoast Tourism Promotions
F. P. I. S.
Harvard, Jolly, Clees, Toppe, Architects, PA, AIA
Hungry Howie's Pizza
Kenny Communications
MEGA - 760
Mercantile Bank/Gulf West Banks, Inc.
National Colorgraphics, Inc.
Publix Super Market Charities
Ruden, McClosky, Smith, Schuster & Russell, P.A.
Travel Host of Tampa Bay
U-92
WDUV–The Dove
Yessawich, Pepperdine & Browne
WFLA-970

The Florida International Museum is sponsored in part by
the State of Florida, Department of State, Division of
Cultural Affairs and the Florida Arts Council.

For Information on upcoming exhibitions, please visit our
web site: www.floridamuseum.org

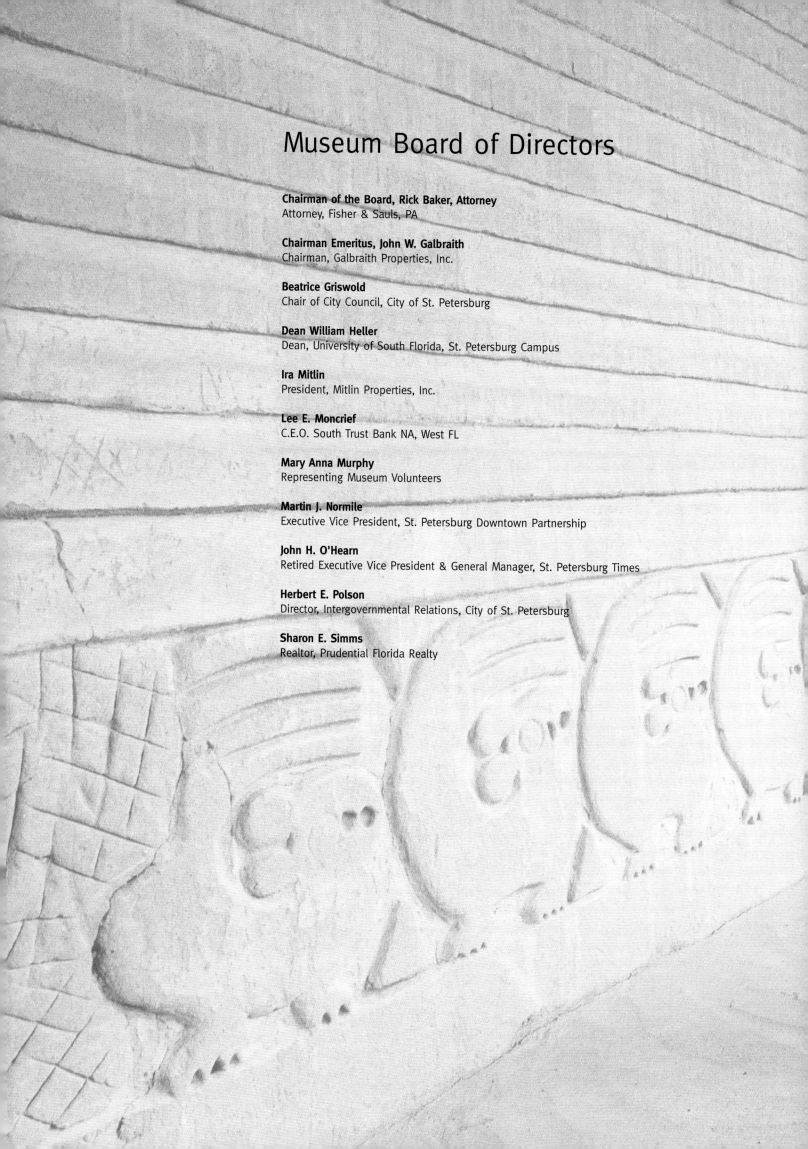

Florida International Museum

Executive Staff
Joseph F. Cronin, *President and C.E.O.*
Pamela Robbins, *Administrative Assistant*
Jennifer Tommasini, *Receptionist*

Architect
Harvard Jolly Clees & Toppe, PA, AIA
Jonathan R. Toppe, AIA, *Principal Exhibition Designer*
Jeff R. Domb, *Designer*
Markus Earley, *Lighting Design*

Building and Gallery Construction
Irwin Contracting, Inc.
Rob Parker, *Project Manager*

Curatorial Service
Steve Masler, *Exhibition Curator*
Vera Espinola, *Museum Curator*

Legal
Ruden, McClosky, Smith, Schuster and Russell
Robert C. Decker

Museum Store
Refaat Hassan, General Manager
Colin Rickerby, Manager

Finance
W. Richard Johnston, *Director*
Renee Richard, *Controller*
Cynthia Erhard, *Accounting Assistant*

Auditors
Gregory, Sharer and Stewart

Insurance
Wallace, Welch and Willingham

Operations
Mark Macksimowicz, *Director*
Amy Barnes, Operations Assistant
Neil Corrado, Building Engineer
Levi Harris, Assistant Building Engineer
Marvin Davisburg, Transportation
Mike Hill, Transportation

Security
Alan Dick, *Director*
Herman Woodburn, Parking Garage

Antenna Theatre
Chris Tellis, *Director of Audio Tours*
Harriet Moss, *Executive Director*
Pamela Desmarais, *Project Manager*

Sally Ruddich, *Writer*
Exhibitions
Sheila Mutchler, *Director*

Volunteer Program
Sharon Jackson, *Coordinator*
Katie Viverette, *Volunteer Assistant*
Windy Crowder, *Volunteer Assistant & Speakers Bureau Coordinator*

Marketing and Public Relations
Wayne David Atherholt, *Director*
Laurel Lynch, *Marketing Coordinator*

Sales
Dannette Lynch, *Manager*
Missy Hahn-Pike, *Hospitality Sales Manger*

Box Office & Reservations
Stacy Boessel, *Box Office Manager*
Lori China, *Box Office Assistant Manager*
Christopher Kruslicky, *Box Office Supervisor*

Public Relations
Mathias "Matt" Bergendahl, *Coordinator*
Sahlman-Williams
  John Williams
  Karen McKinney
Destination Counselors, Inc.

Advertising & Marketing Firms
Yessawich, Pepperdine and Brown
  Cedar Hames
  Dave DiMaggio
  Glenn Horn
Creative Solutions, Inc.
  Art Fyvolent
  Corky Miller
  Tracy Dodd
National Colorgraphics, Inc.
  Christine Tabor

Catalogue Production
Federico Kauffmann-Doig, Text
Eulogio Guzmán, Translation
Lithograph Publishing Company, a division of Lithograph Printing Company
  Russ Gordon, *Project Manager*
  Connie Reeves, *Production Coordinator*
Garrett White, *Editing and Design*

Introduction

With a lust for gold and the desire to make a name for himself, the strong-willed Francisco Pizzaro (1478–1541), already a wealthy landowner in Panama as a result of his exploits as an invading Spanish soldier in the New World, led three expeditions with the intent of conquering the Incas and claiming their wealth for himself and for Spain.

In 1532, Francisco Pizarro and his band of 260 conquistadors headed toward the city of Cajamarca to confront the last ruler of the Inca empire. Along their way, the Spanish invaders confirmed the stories they had heard in Panama, until now considered too fantastic, about the legendary land of gold that lay to the south. But they were astonished by more than an abundance of gold. They were equally amazed to find that the country was governed by a meticulously planned administration, reflecting the presence of a highly evolved culture. Although the forms of this culture were alien, many of its achievements were comparable in scale to those of Spain, and in some cases surpassed them, as demonstrated by the superb Inca highway system on which the conquerors traveled. Using labor contributed as a form of tax, the Incas built more than 20,000 miles of paved highway. Extending some 3,000 miles down the length of the empire, from southern Chile to what is now northern Ecuador, the complex system—reserved for elites—included suspended bridges, rest areas, and strategically placed quarters for eating and lodging. Ironically, these roads enormously facilitated the movement of Pizzaro's army, which included sixty-two horsemen and two pieces of artillery provided by the king of Spain.

The Spanish were astounded when they reached impressive monuments like Sacsahuaman in the Inca capital of Cuzco. In 1534, Pedro Sancho, Pizarro's secretary, related without exaggeration that "many Spanish who had seen and walked in Lombardy and in other strange kingdoms said that they had never seen an edifice like this fortress, nor stronger castles . . . of such great stones that no one who had seen them would say that they had been put there by human hands."

Even as they plundered its riches, the Spanish were awed by the achievements of the Inca empire in statecraft and monumental architecture, and conscious of the fact that they had encountered an advanced civilization. But Inca civilization did not evolve overnight. The earliest monumental architecture in ancient Peru was approximately contemporary with the pyramids of Egypt, and the Central Andes is one of the few regions on earth in which a true civilization—characterized in part by highly developed agricultural systems, technical advancements in art and metallurgy, the stratification of society into classes, and the building of complex cities and states—arose without significant contact with more advanced cultures. Although short-lived, the Inca empire, which contained more than ten million people at its height, was the culmination of thousands of years of development throughout the Central Andes.

This fact has only been fully recognized through modern archaeology, in part because the Incas

Inca highway engineers met the challenge presented by deep river gorges with suspended bridges. This modern reconstruction was made with 22,000 feet of hand-braided ichu *grass, and secured to the original stone pediments set by the Incas.*

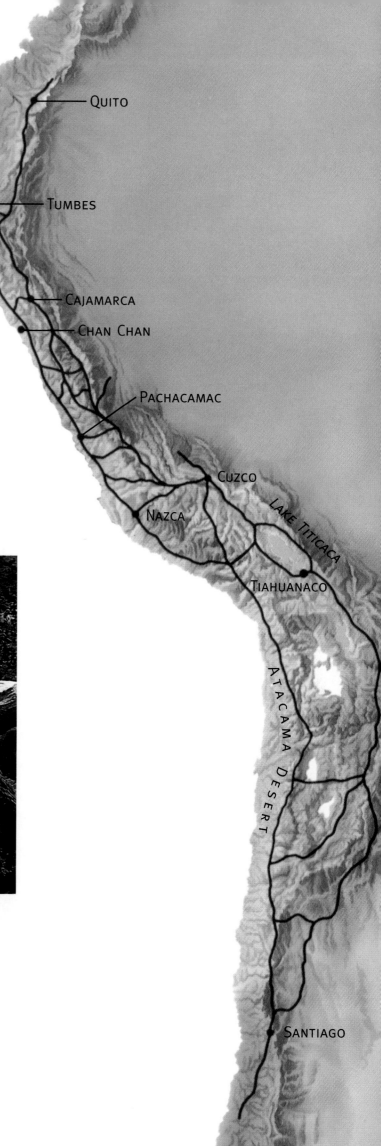

QUITO

TUMBES

CAJAMARCA

CHAN CHAN

PACHACAMAC

CUZCO

NAZCA

LAKE TITICACA

TIAHUANACO

ATACAMA DESERT

SANTIAGO

Gold Mask of the Sicán Lord Naymlap
Sicán (Lambayeque) (A.D. 700–1370)
Height: 22 cm (8.6 in) Width: 28 cm (11 in)
National Museum of Archaeology, Anthropology and
History of Peru, Lima

*(Below) A section of surviving Inca roadway at 15,000 feet in
the sierra above Lima.*

themselves had successfully propagated a mythology that placed them at the inception of Andean civilization. Post-conquest elaboration of that mythology decisively influenced early chroniclers and historians, and it wasn't until near the turn of this century that a fuller picture of the origins of Andean civilization began to emerge.

For thousands of years before the dominance of the Incas—then a specific ethnic group comprised of as few as 40,000—many other groups in Peru had achieved great power and created spectacular art and architecture. Cities and empires had risen, flourished, then disappeared. Yet despite the sudden demise of these cultures, technology and artistic traditions were passed on through the centuries. Widespread cultural exchange has been traced back to the florescence of the Chavín civilization in the first millennium B.C. Pre-Hispanic Andean culture never developed a written language, but legends, myths, and historical

Double burial excavated in the Preceramic Period site of Panaulauca Cave in the central puna of Peru. Dating to about 3500 B.C., this formally positioned aged woman (right) and sprawled teenage girl were buried together under circumstances we can only guess at.

Hunter-gatherers lived in Panaulauca Cave from at least 8000 B.C. until perhaps 1800 B.C., building up an enormous mass of debris in the cave mouth. Excavations here have revealed evidence of people who intensely hunted the llama-like vicuña.

Rock art probably made by hunter-gatherers of the Preceramic Period (pre-1800 B.C.) in the cave site of Cuchimachay in the high sierra puna above Lima. The animals are undoubtedly members of the camelid family, which includes the llama; these may be vicuña, a favorite prey of early hunters.

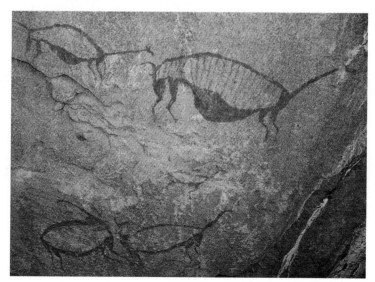

(Above, left to right) Pitcher in the Form of a Seated Man
Height: 23 cm (9.2 in) Diameter: 21 cm (8.1 in)

Pitcher in the Form of a Man of High Status
Height: 24 cm (9.5 in) Diameter: 14 cm (5.5 in)

Pitcher in the Form of a Young Man of High Rank
Height: 25 cm (9.9 in) Diameter: 15 cm (5.9 in)

Ceramic
Moche (A.D. 50–800)
National Museum of Archaeology, Anthropology and
History of Peru, Lima

*The Moche continued to produce difficult to make and easily
breakable stirrup-spout pitchers like those above because of
the symbolic link with their Cupisnique and Chavín
ancestors. These earlier cultures invested the stirrup spout
with strong religious significance, which may explain why
they often took the form of effigy vessels. In addition to face
portrait vessels, the Moche produced full-figure pitchers of
human effigies, which, while focusing on social status, also
hint at characteristic behaviors. The three figures depicted
above are all of high social rank, as evidenced by their ear
ornaments, emblems, and soft-cloth turbans. The position of
the full-form male figure shown above left, seated in a
traditional pose with crossed legs and hands on his knees,
suggests that he may be giving orders. The ear ornaments on
the elite individual depicted in the center vessel are similar to
gold ornaments discovered in Moche tombs. The earlobes
were pierced and elongated to accommodate the enormous
earrings, which were supported at the top by a thin cord. The
vessel on the right depicts a youth of high rank seated with
crossed legs. This figure wears the classic Moche turban
composed of two cloths, one of which wraps around the
head while the other is fastened at the base of the chin. One
hand rests on the figure's knee, while the other is placed at
the chest as if to call attention to the emblem depicted there.*

Pitcher with Motifs Representing Ocean Waves
Height: 7 cm (2.9 in) Diameter: 18 cm (7 in)

Pitcher with Decoration Representing the Body of a Bird
Height: 18 cm (6.9 in) Diameter: 19 cm (7.5 in)

Ceramic
Paracas-Cavernas (700 B.C.–A.D. 1)
National Museum of Archaeology, Anthropology and
History of Peru, Lima

*The bird image on the pitcher shown above right was
painted after the clay had been fired. This technique was
often employed by the Paracas. After firing, vessels were
painted with a variety of colors created by mixing mineral
pigments with plant resin. A bird head, sculpted in clay,
appears on the handle of the vessel. The vessel on the left is
also the product of post-fire decorative techniques. Its
incised surface features a painted geometric design
representing a wave.*

Carved Wooden Ceremonial Oar
Chincha (A.D. 1200–1450)
Width: 21 cm (8.2 in) Length: 19 cm (7.5 in)
National Museum of Archaeology, Anthropology and
History of Peru, Lima

(Below left) Paccha in the Form of a Bowl
Height: 17 cm (6.7 in) Diameter: 17 cm (6.7 in)

Paccha in the Form of a Copulating Couple
Height: 18 cm (7.1 in) Diameter: 18 cm (6.7 in)

Ceramic
Recuay (A.D. 1–650)
National Museum of Archaeology, Anthropology and
History of Peru, Lima

*The positive and negative polychromed vessel shown below
left is partially sculpted, and has a flared rim. This type of
vessel, known by the Quechua name* paccha, *was likely used
in rain rituals and in offerings in which sacred water was
poured through the spout to fertilize the earth. Another
paccha-style vessel, below right, depicts a sculpted
copulation scene. Two smaller women carrying glasses serve
as attendants. White clay, abundant in the northern sierra, is
particular to most Recuay ceramics. Recuay pieces not made
from white clay were most often made from terracotta, then
painted with a coating of white slip paint to create the
illusion of white clay. Sculpted figures in Recuay pieces tend
to be abstract and relatively formless.*

accounts were recorded in elaborately painted
ceramic vessels. Sculptured portraits of warriors,
healers, beggars, and those ravaged by disease
were portrayed in pottery. Animals of the forest and
puna—the high, arid plateaus that are among the
salient features of the diverse Andean
topography—fruits and vegetables from terraced
fields, serpents, crabs, felines, and fish were
brought to vivid life in wood, clay, silver, and gold,
or depicted in elaborately twined textiles.

The Distant Past

The territory of ancient Peru had been well traveled
for more than 10,000 years before the advent of
the Spanish on Inca lands. At Lauricocha, an
archaeological site situated at an altitude of 13,000
feet in the central sierra, caves have been found in
which the first Peruvians found shelter. In the
southern extreme, they also took refuge in caves,
such as those at Toquepala. The cultural evidence
at both sites is confined largely to projectile points
chipped in stone. The walls of Toquepala's caves

(Above) Tripod Bowls
(Left) Height: 17 cm (6.7 in) Diameter: 17 cm (6.7 in)
(Right) Height: 8 cm (3.3 in) Diameter: 16 cm (6.3 in)

Ceramic
Cajamarca (A.D. 200–800)
National Museum of Archaeology, Anthropology and
History of Peru, Lima

*The meaning of the patterns on these pieces is unknown.
The spiral shapes inside the brightly colored bowl above left
represent ocean waves. The inside of the bowl above right is
illustrated with an image of a supernatural owl-faced figure.*

(Right) Stirrup-Spout Pitchers
(Left) Height: 17 cm (6.7 in) Diameter: 14 cm (5.5 in)
(Right) Height: 23 cm (9 in) Diameter: 17 cm (6.7 in)

Ceramic
Cupisnique (1000 B.C.–A.D. 200)
National Museum of Archaeology, Anthropology and
History of Peru, Lima

*The north coast Cupisnique culture produced some of the
most refined ceramics in ancient Peru. The monochromatic
piece at far right features motifs that symbolize raindrops.
The dark color of the vessel at right is the result of firing in a
closed oven. The ornamental motif is an ocean wave.*

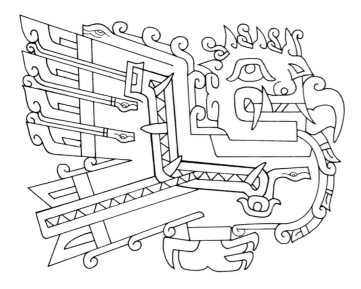

were painted with hunting scenes that date to the early hunting and gathering period.

The most remote ancestors of the Incas were hunters and food gatherers. Primitive groups along the Pacific coast were especially adept at extracting marine products from the rich coastal waters. They were the descendants of the groups originating in Asia who crossed the Bering land bridge into North America during the last ice age. These early Asiatic peoples dispersed throughout the continent, carrying with them from their native lands the intrinsic cultural traditions that, by the second millennium B.C., would evolve into the first significant Andean civilizations.

The Initial Sparks of Civilization

During the second millennium B.C., several thousand years after the occupation of the region, the first signs of a civilization began to emerge in Peru, in some cases following a shift from hunting and gathering to intensive marine exploitation and then to agriculture. One result of this early manifestation of a more complex social structure was increased population growth, which in turn necessitated a search for improved irrigation, growing, and food storage techniques.

Architectural evidence best characterizes the beginnings of a civilization. Enormous monuments began to rise along the central coast and in the northern region of Peru. Las Haldas, for example (ca. 1800 B.C.), is a vast Preceramic site on the north coast that included living areas as well as ceremonial and communal centers. Early

Pitcher with Symbolic Representations of Terraced Fields
Ceramic
Nazca (A.D. 1–700)
Height: 18 cm (7.1 in) Diameter: 13 cm (5.1 in)
National Museum of Archaeology, Anthropology and History of Peru, Lima

This red, black, and white slip-painted polychrome vessel is decorated with a step-fret motif.

(Top left) Line drawing of an eagle carved into the cornice of a stone portal at Chavín de Huántar.

The dry puna grasslands of central Peru, at an altitude of nearly 14,000 feet, were made useful to early cultures through the domestication of grazing camelids such as the llama and alpaca.

monumental public architecture emerged in Peru as a result of the desires of elites, who apparently benefitted from the construction of these imposing edifices. Essentially religious in nature, such structures elevated the prestige of the elites, and assured that their orders would be carefully obeyed. The rule of the elites was aimed primarily at increasing their own privileges by gaining preferred access to resources. Secondarily, their rule was directed toward maintenance of the community, and guaranteeing adequate food production.

The Central Andean region contains several of the harshest and most formidable environments on earth. The long story of the rise and fall of ancient civilizations in Peru is closely connected to the unusually varied and severe geography, which includes the arid Peruvian coast, interrupted only by occasional narrow rivers; the Andean cordillera, which reaches 22,000 feet at its highest peak; the vast puna; the highland valleys, with their abrupt slopes and limited cultivable soils; and the dense tropical forests of the eastern Andean slopes that descend into the Amazon basin. Each of these environments, along with periodic natural disasters such as major earthquakes, and dramatic changes in climate and food supply brought on by the El Niño current, acted as powerful stimulants toward the development of increasingly complex strategies for survival.

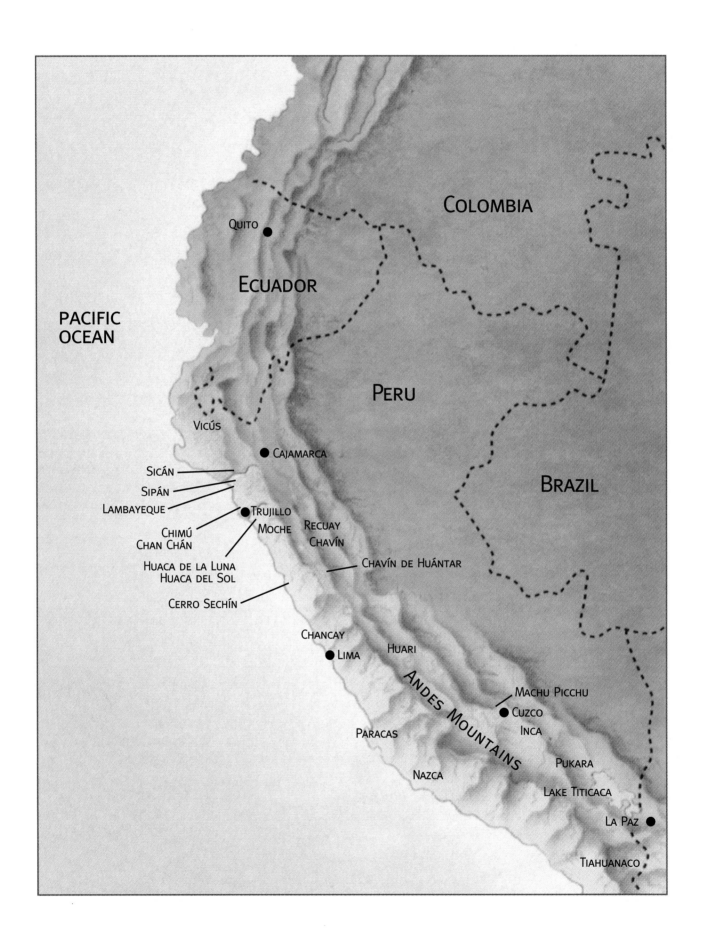

COLOMBIA

Quito

ECUADOR

PACIFIC
OCEAN

PERU

Vicús

Cajamarca

BRAZIL

Sicán
Sipán
Lambayeque
Chimú
Chan Chán

Trujillo
Moche

Recuay
Chavín

Huaca de la Luna
Huaca del Sol

Chavín de Huántar

Cerro Sechín

Chancay

Huari

Lima

ANDES MOUNTAINS

Machu Picchu

Cuzco
Inca

Paracas

Pukara

Nazca

Lake Titicaca

La Paz

Tiahuanaco

Introduction

	World Events	North Coast	North Highlands	Central Coast	Central Highlands	South Coast	South Highlands	Relative Chronology
AD 1600								
AD 1532		INCA 1200–1532	INCA 1200–1532	INCA 1200–1532	INCA 1200–1532	INCA 1200–1532	INCA 1200–1532	LATE HORIZON 1450-1532
AD 1517	PROTESTANT REFORMATION							
AD 1492	COLUMBUS DISCOVERS NEW WORLD							
		CHIMÚ 1100–1450		CHANCAY 1200–1450 CHINCHA 1200–1450				LATE INTERMEDIATE PERIOD 1000–1450
AD 1215	MAGNA CARTA SIGNED BY KING JOHN OF ENGLAND	SICÁN (LAMBAYEQUE) 700–1370						
AD 1066	NORMAN CONQUEST OF ENGLAND							MIDDLE HORIZON 650–1000
	CHINESE INVENT GUNPOWDER, 1000							
AD 800		MOCHE 50–800	CAJAMARCA 200–800 RECUAY 1–650		HUARI 650–800		TIAHUANACO 200–800	
AD 700						NAZCA 1–700		EARLY INTERMEDIATE PERIOD 1–650
AD 635	RISE OF ARAB EMPIRE MOHAMMED, 570–632							
	MAYAN GOLDEN AGE							
AD 476	FALL OF ROME							
AD 226	SASSINIAN EMPIRE IN PERSIA							
AD 200		VICÚS 200 BC–200		LIMA 200–600			PUKARA 200 BC–200	
AD 44	ASSASSINATION OF JULIUS CAESAR, 44 BC ROMANS CONQUER BRITAIN, 43 BC							
0						PARACAS 700 BC–1		EARLY HORIZON 700–1
140 BC	VENUS DE MILO							
200 BC		CUPISNIQUE 1000–200 BC	CHAVÍN DE HUÁNTAR 1000–200 BC					
326 BC	ALEXANDER THE GREAT CONQUERS EGYPT AND WESTERN ASIA, 336–323 BC							
	BUDDHA, 565–483 BC							
538 BC	PERSIAN EMPIRE, 538–333 BC							
776 BC	FIRST OLYMPIC GAMES							
875 BC	AGE OF THE HEBREW PROPHETS, 875–520 BC							
1000 BC								INITIAL PERIOD

The Natural World

The accomplishments of Andean culture are all the more remarkable given the harsh natural environment in which it flourished. That the people of the Andes survived and thrived in a geographic region marked by extremes says much about their resourceful ingenuity and flexibility. Peru is indeed a land of contrasts, encompassing three distinct land forms with varied ecosystems: the Andes mountains, surpassed in scale only by the Himalayas; the Amazonian lowlands; and the arid Pacific coast. The sea floor off the coast of Peru moves eastward, sliding under the westward-moving continent at a rate of 3 to 12 inches per year. This causes buckling at the continental margin, forming the rugged Andes. The cold waters of the Humboldt current sweep northward from the Antarctic along 2,000 miles of Peruvian coast, which supports one of the richest marine food chains in the world. The cold Humboldt does not, however, bring moisture to the air. As a result, what should be a tropical coast, given its proximity to the equator, is in fact the driest in the world, with most areas receiving little or no significant rainfall.

A narrow strip of desert intersected by dozens of small rivers, many of which are seasonally dry, the coastal plain varies from approximately 12.5 to 30 miles in width, broadening to 60 miles in the north and almost disappearing in the south. Despite the arid climate, ancient Peruvians first settled the coast to make use of the abundant marine resources. Stable cities did not appear, however, until after agriculture was introduced to the

Short horizontal distances in the Andes can involve enormous altitude changes, as seen in this view of the Cordillera Blanca (White Sierra) of north-central Peru. The snowcapped peaks in the distance tower above 21,000 feet; the foreground valley lies below 10,000 feet.

(Opposite) Pitcher Representing a Messenger of the God Aiapaec
Moche (A.D. 50–800) Height: 27 cm (10.7 in) Diameter: 26 cm (10.3 in)
National Museum of Archaeology, Anthropology and History of Peru, Lima

The insignia and headdress on this figure associate it with Aiapaec, the Moche god of the mountains and rivers. He wears a loincloth, and a collar. Similar collars, made of hollow spheres of gold, have been found in Moche tombs. He also wears a semicircular headdress with a feline head at its center. Superimposed on the feline head is the emblem of a bird.

region. Experiments in irrigation were begun more than four thousand years ago, and the coastal river valleys were eventually laced with man-made canals. While most of these water conduits were functional, some appear to be too ornate or insubstantial to have served a practical purpose. It is believed, however, that they may have been built with the intent of ritually manipulating rainfall and runoff.

Given the region's moderate year-round temperatures, almost any crop could be cultivated in the fertile soils. By 1000 B.C., the coastal valleys were filling up with agricultural communities. The coastal valleys supported a series of outstanding civilizations, including the Vicús, Moche, Chimú, Chancay, Paracas, and Nazca. Important architectural remains have been found from each of these cultures. These include the group of pyramids from Túcume and Batán Grande; the great Chimú city of Chan Chán; the truncated Moche pyramids of the sun and the moon—known as Huaca de la Luna and Huaca del Sol—and the ruins of Pachacámac and Cajamarquilla, as well as stupendous examples of textiles, ceramics, and gold. Among the most prolific and artistically gifted of these cultures were the Moche. Excellent painters and clay sculptors, they left an invaluable iconographic

(Top left) Pitcher in the Form of a Coiled Serpent
Ceramic
Lima (A.D. 200–600)
Height: 15 cm (5.9 in) Diameter: 14 cm (5.5 in)
National Museum of Archaeology, Anthropology and History of Peru, Lima

(Left) Pitcher with Relief Images of Deer Struck by Lances
Ceramic
Moche (A.D. 50–800)
Height: 21 cm (7.9 in) Diameter: 16 cm (6.3 in)
National Museum of Archaeology, Anthropology and History of Peru, Lima

(Above, left to right) Pitcher in the Form of a Feline Head
Height: 23 cm (9.1 in) Diameter: 22 cm (8.7 in)

Pitcher in the Form of Two Copulating Rodents
Height: 22 cm (8.7 in) Diameter: 23 cm (9.1 in)

Pitcher with Relief Images of Feline Heads
Height: 26 cm (10.2 in) Diameter: 16 cm (6.3 in)

Ceramic
Moche (A.D. 50–800)
National Museum of Archaeology, Anthropology and
History of Peru, Lima

*Felines adorn the vessels shown above left and above right.
The vessel above center depicts two rodents copulating on
a throne. The male appears to be offering the female a
peanut.*

*(Right) At 14,000 feet, the puna grasslands of Peru comprise
14 percent of the entire region. Extending from Ecuador to
Chile, they frequently form high plains between the major
ranges of the Andes.*

(Above, left to right) Pitcher in the Form of a Llama
Height: 18 cm (7.1 in) Diameter: 18 cm (7.1 in)

Pitcher in the Form of a Grazing Llama with Symbolic Motifs
Height: 15 cm (5.9 in) Diameter: 21 cm (8.3 in)

Pitcher in the Form of a Feline with Symbolic Motifs
Height: 16 cm (6.3 in) Diameter: 18 cm (7.1 in)

Ceramic
Tiahuanaco-Huari (A.D. 200–800)
National Museum of Archaeology, Anthropology and
History of Peru, Lima

*Many symbolic motifs adorn each of these vessels, from a
repetitive geometric design in the form of concentric circles
and joined triangles, to bird and water imagery.*

The Natural World

The Casma Valley (above) on the north central coast of Peru. The stark sand and rock desert of the rainless coast breaks into productive green valleys wherever irrigation waters extend. These valley oases can produce great quantities of agricultural products.

In the coastal foggy season, peaking around August, moist air fosters the growth of lush, verdant plant life on the hills at around 1,000 feet. This fog meadow, or loma (opposite), as this type of landscape is known in Peru, lies just north of the Moche Valley city of Trujillo. During the coastal sunny season that runs from December to April, the fog meadows disappear completely. At left is the same hill slope six months later.

Paccha in the Form of a Fish
Ceramic
Chimú (A.D. 1100–1450)
Length: 39 cm (15.1 in) Diameter: 8 cm (3.1 in)
National Museum of Archaeology, Anthropology and
History of Peru, Lima

*This monochrome fish-shaped paccha was a ritual object
intended to make the earth fertile.*

Sculpted Shell
Ceramic
Moche (A.D. 50–800)
Height: 29 cm (11.4 in) Diameter: 14 cm (5.5 in)
National Museum of Archaeology, Anthropology and
History of Peru, Lima

*This sculpture is a ceramic reproduction of a marine conch
used as a trumpet or* pututo. *The pututo was also used to
send signals to messengers. Ancient chroniclers, such as
Bernabé Cobo, tell us that the conch was considered the
offspring of the sea, suggesting an association with rain-
related rituals. The pututo is still used in the Cuzco region.*

record about Moche culture, and especially about the coastal area in which they lived.

The labor and creativity that these Andean cultures invested in overcoming their environment could be undone by a single earthquake or climatic disaster. For centuries, Andean civilizations have contended with a pattern of devastating climatic reversals caused by the periodic replacement of the cold Humboldt current by a warm current. Called El Niño, the Spanish nickname for the Christ child, the current is usually first noticed around Christmas. Its effects can be far-reaching. During a significant El Niño, areas in the southern mountains that normally have moderate rainfall experience drought, and torrential rains flood the desert coast. The warmer waters kill plankton, causing marine wildlife to migrate. And while a normal El Niño can last a year to eighteen months, there is evidence that in

Pitcher Depicting a Fish
Ceramic
Chimú (A.D. 1100–1450)
Height: 21 cm (8.3 in) Diameter: 21 cm (8.3 in)
National Museum of Archaeology, Anthropology and History of Peru, Lima

While the Moche used molds to create their sculpture chambers, the Chimú went a step further and used molds to make the stirrup spouts as well. A small creature is depicted at the base of the spout on this fish-shaped pitcher.

Pitcher Depicting a School of Fish
Ceramic
Nazca (A.D. 1–700)
Height: 18 cm (7.1 in) Diameter: 14 cm (5.5 in)
National Museum of Archaeology, Anthropology and History of Peru, Lima

Swimming fish are painted over the base of this double-spouted polychromed vessel. Incised lines, which had earlier outlined the colored areas of proto-Nazca art pieces, were later replaced by thin black lines, such as those shown here. This practice of black slip outlining became a prominent feature of Nazca art.

(Top left) Pitcher in the Form of a Bird Carrying a Feline
Ceramic
Moche (A.D. 50–800)
Height: 22 cm (8.7 in) Diameter: 23 cm (9.1 in)

(Top right) Pitcher Depicting a Monkey Eating Fruit
Ceramic
Chimú (A.D. 1100–1450)
Height: 19 cm (7.5 in) Diameter: 18 cm (7.1 in)

National Museum of Archaeology, Anthropology and
History of Peru, Lima

*The Moche vessel at top left depicts the unusual scene of a
bird in flight with a feline on its back. Monkeys similar to the
one shown top right are a prominent feature of Chimú art.*

(Center left) Pitcher Depicting Warriors and Weapons
with Symbolic Images
Height: 28 cm (11 in) Diameter: 15 cm (5.9 in)

(Center right) Pitcher Depicting Rows of Snails
Height: 29 cm (11.4 in) Diameter: 16 cm (6.3 in)

Ceramic
Moche (A.D. 50–800)
National Museum of Archaeology, Anthropology and
History of Peru, Lima

*The scenes painted on these stirrup-spout bottles show
movement. On the vessel at far left, three warriors rush to
battle carrying clubs. At left, snails travel across fields
represented by horizontal lines.*

(Bottom left) Incised Bowl with Feline Face
Height: 12 cm (5 in) Diameter: 20 cm (7.8 in)

(Bottom right) Wind Instrument with Feline Head
Length: 23 cm (9.1 in)

Ceramic
Pukara (200 B.C.–A.D. 200)
National Museum of Archaeology, Anthropology and
History of Peru, Lima

*(Opposite, top) The steep cultivated slopes of the upper
Mosna Valley above Chavín de Huántar in the north central
highlands. Fields like these in the highland valleys of Peru
rely on rain water.*

*(Opposite, bottom) Looking coastward from the sierra
above Lima, the ever-narrowing Rimac coastal valley cuts
through the dry Andes hills. In the distance lies the fog bank
typical of the coastal overcast season.*

the past some have lasted much longer, killing marine wildlife, destroying crops for successive years, and causing widespread famine. There is also evidence that major cities were abandoned due to severe drought and food shortages brought on by El Niño. In fact, many of the civilizations that arose in Peru vanished suddenly from the archaeological record.

The steep, jagged Andes run north-south along the western edge of South America from Colombia and Venezuela to Cape Horn. The highest point in Peru is 22,205-foot Huascarán. Crowned by perpetual snow, with high plateaus and glacial lakes, inter-Andean basins, and deep ravines, the mountainous chains, called cordilleras, frequently have highland valleys or high plains between them. At an average altitude of 14,000 feet, this is the Altiplano, the best grazing land in Peru. The Inca and their ancestors emphasized the farming

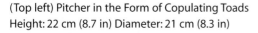

(Top left) Pitcher in the Form of Copulating Toads
Height: 22 cm (8.7 in) Diameter: 21 cm (8.3 in)

(Bottom left) Pitcher Depicting a Boy Reclining on the
Back of a Llama
Height: 22 cm (8.7 in) Diameter: 20 cm (7.9 in)

Ceramic
Moche (A.D. 50–800)
National Museum of Archaeology, Anthropology and
History of Peru, Lima

*While many animals in Moche art are often
anthropomorphized or portrayed with the limbs or body parts
of humans and other animals, llamas are usually depicted
realistically. Here, a llama carries a bundle on each side, and a
boy reclines on its back.*

*(Left) The canals of the Cumbemayo site in the northern
sierra near Cajamarca. These rock-cut water channels may
date to the Early Horizon. Their small capacity suggests that
they may have served a ritual purpose.*

(Top right) Pitcher Representing a Feline with
Supernatural Markings
Height: 20 cm (7.9 in) Diameter: 19 cm (7.5 in)

(Bottom right) Pitcher in the Form of a Bound Llama and
its Owner
Height: 21 cm (8.3 in) Diameter: 24 cm (9.4 in)

Ceramic
Moche (A.D. 50–800)
National Museum of Archaeology, Anthropology and
History of Peru, Lima

*The pitcher at top right depicts a sculpted feline with
markings associated with the supernatural. The spout on
the monochromatic vessel at bottom right is a sculpted
human figure. The chamber depicts a South American
camelid, perhaps a llama, lying with its limbs tied.*

(Above, left to right) Pitcher Depicting a Mythical Deer
Suckling a Fawn
Height: 22 cm (8.7 in) Diameter: 18 cm (7.5 in)

Pitcher Depicting a Feline Attacking a Deer
Height: 21 cm (8.3 in) Diameter: 15 cm (5.9 in)

Pitcher Depicting a Deer at Rest
Height: 21 cm (8.3 in) Diameter: 24 cm (9.4 in)

Ceramic
Moche (A.D. 50–800)
National Museum of Archaeology, Anthropology and
History of Peru, Lima

(Left) Bowl Depicting Monkeys
Ceramic
Nazca (A.D. 1–700)
Height: 8 cm (3.2 in) Diameter: 19 cm (7.5 in)
National Museum of Archaeology, Anthropology and
History of Peru, Lima

The Natural World

(Above, left to right) Pitcher Depicting Wading Birds Hunting Snails
Height: 24 cm (9.4 in) Diameter: 23 cm (9.1 in)

Pitcher Depicting Lizards
Height: 23 cm (9.1 in) Diameter: 16 cm (6.3 in)

Pitcher Depicting Water Plants, Fish, and Snails
Height: 23 cm (9.1 in) Diameter: 17 cm (6.7 in)

Ceramic
Moche (A.D. 50–800)
National Museum of Archaeology, Anthropology and
History of Peru, Lima

(Right) Cup with Images of Severed Heads
Ceramic
Nazca (A.D. 1–700)
Height: 11 cm (4.4 in) Diameter: 16 cm (6.3 in)
National Museum of Archaeology, Anthropology and
History of Peru, Lima

The Cordillera Blanca range towers above puna grasslands in the upper reaches of the Callejón de Huaylas, the drainage of the Santa River in north central Peru. Chavín de Huántar lies beyond the snowcaps in the distance.

of the highland valley zones, although some higher regions were also utilized. Steep mountains were terraced, and crops especially resistant to extremes of cold and lack of oxygen were cultivated there. Llama and alpaca may have been domesticated by five thousand years ago, and grazed on the puna grasslands, which were too high to sustain crops. The camelids native to the region, which, in addition to llamas and alpacas, include the wild vicuña and guanaco, have been a great resource to the Andean people, serving as pack animals on the rough terrain, and providing fiber for textiles, leather and bone for tools, and meat. Below the puna zone is the *suni* zone with steep slopes

and hollows where tubers and grains were grown. The *quechua* zone is comprised of the lower slopes and valley floor. Here a great number of vegetables were cultivated, often with the help of irrigation. Ravines and intermediate or *chaupiyunga* zones were exploited for the cultivation of fruit trees and temperate-zone crops.

Lake Titicaca, situated at 12,508 feet, is a freshwater basin that covers an area of 3,200 square miles, of which approximately 60 percent lies in Peru and the remainder in Bolivia. Its maximum depth is 650 feet, and it is characterized by a shallow shoreline. Titicaca's waters crest to waves of 1.6 feet with tide changes of up to 2.6 feet. The lake's waters also

(Below) Ceramic Bowls with Feline-Head Handles and Motifs Depicting Edible Plants

Tiahuanaco-Huari (A.D. 200–800)
Height: 59 cm (23.2 in) Diameter: 88 cm (34.6 in)
National Museum of Archaeology, Anthropology and History of Peru, Lima

These urns feature handles in the shape of feline heads. The polychrome decorations on the exterior and rim surfaces display motifs in the form of potatoes and corn. Urns such as these are among the most impressive of Huari ceramics.

(Below) Ceramic Pitcher with Geometric Motifs

Inca (A.D. 1200–1532)
Height: 110 cm (43.3 in) Diameter: 65 cm (25.7 in) (right)
National Museum of Archaeology, Anthropology and History of Peru, Lima

Large Aribalo pitchers like this were used to store and serve liquids, such as the corn-based alcoholic beverage chicha. Ancient Peruvians attached cords to the handles and carried these vessels on their backs. This type of bottle is reminiscent of the Greek Aribalo vessel, hence its name.

(Below left and above right) Ceramic Corn Stalk
Height: 26 cm (10.2 in) Diameter: 12 cm (4.7 in)

(Above left) Pitcher in the Form of Edible Fruit
Height: 11 cm (4.5 in) Diameter: 18 cm (7 in)

Ceramic
Nazca (A.D. 1–700)
National Museum of Archaeology, Anthropology and
History of Peru, Lima

*The ears of corn on these sculpted stalks are depicted
without husks. White lines illustrate the stems and roots of
the stalks. The vessel above left represents a pair of* lúcuma, *a
fruit native to Peru and widely consumed since ancient times.*

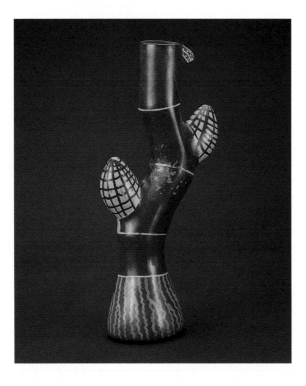

The Natural World

(Below, left to right) Pitcher Depicting Grain Buds and Stylized Severed Heads
Height: 19 cm (7.5 in) Diameter: 16 cm (6.3 in)

Pitcher Depicting Beans and Stylized Severed Heads
Height: 19 cm (7.5 in) Diameter: 17 cm (6.7 in)

Pitcher Depicting Food of Earth and Sea
Height: 13 cm (5.1 in) Diameter: 13 cm (5.1 in)

Bowl Depicting Peppers
Height: 8 cm (3.2 in) Diameter: 21 cm (8.3 in)

Ceramic
Nazca (A.D. 1–700)
National Museum of Archaeology, Anthropology and History of Peru, Lima

Food is featured on each of the objects shown below. Beans, chiles, corn, and fish are among the more recognizable edibles. The pattern on the third vessel from left features a type of jíquima *that has since become extinct.*

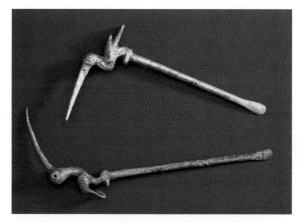

Silver Spatula with a Bird Image (Above, top)
Height: 7 cm (2.7 in) Length: 4 cm (1.6 in)

Silver Spatula with a Bird Image Inlaid with Spondylus Shell (Above, bottom)
Height: 9 cm (3.5 in) Length: 4 cm (1.6 in)

Inca (A.D. 1200–1532)
National Museum of Archaeology, Anthropology and History of Peru, Lima

Copper and silver spatulas such as these were used to extract small amounts of lime or ash from gourds. The lime was mixed with coca leaves and chewed to provide energy and alleviate symptoms of altitude sickness.

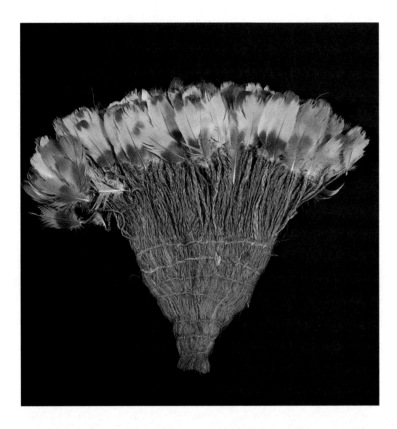

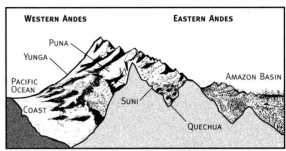

modify the climate of the high plateau, raising temperatures on cold nights, and alleviating the severity of dryness in the puna zones.

Archaeological evidence from different eras of Peruvian civilization is abundant in the Titicaca basin, including the monumental architecture of Tiahuanaco, ruins from the Pukara and Huari cultures, and the burial towers, known as *chullpas*, of Sillustani, which stand near the shores of Lake Titicaca.

In contrast to the arid plateaus and valleys of the western slopes and central highlands, there is heavy rainfall on the lush eastern slopes from September through April, with almost no precipitation during the rest of the year. There are few forests, except in the Amazon Andes, where the eastern slope is covered by tropical vegetation. There, potatoes and quinoa could be grown near the mountaintops, and manioc and tropical fruits were grown on the jungle floor, but the rugged terrain of the eastern slopes was not conducive to farming. A wide variety of unique flora and fauna thrives in the inter-Andean basins and high plateaus. Animals commonly depicted on

Feather Fans
Nazca (A.D. 1–700)
Width: 32 cm (12.5 in) Length: 25 cm (9.8 in) (top left)
Width: 29 cm (11.3 in) Length: 38 cm (14.8 in) (bottom left)
National Museum of Archaeology, Anthropology and History of Peru, Lima

Weaving composed of vegetable fiber braids serves as the base for the feather fan at top left. Coiled strings fasten feathers to a cane to create the fan at bottom left.

Andean ceramics, textiles, and sculpture include vicuñas, llamas, and alpacas, apes and monkeys, the antejo bear, pumas, and jaguars, as well as toucans and the majestic condor, which also inhabits the coast.

A distinction is made between high Amazon, or high jungle, and low Amazon. These are known, respectively, as the Amazon Andes and Amazonia. The Amazon Andes is characterized by tropical forests with fog conditions, while the Amazon is distinguished by rain forest. Contact between the eco-regions of the Andes and the Amazon region, which today occupies 60 percent of Peru, has existed for thousands of years. Amazon plants like the yucca were cultivated in the coastal Andes, and there was extensive trade, including the wide exchange of colorful feathers from the Amazon region for finely worked stone and metal axes from the Andes.

The cultures of the Amazon Andes settled at altitudes of approximately 6,500 feet. The

(Above, left to right) Pitcher Depicting a Supernatural Being in the Form of a Killer Whale
Height: 16 cm (6.4 in) Diameter: 13 cm (5.2 in)

Pitcher Depicting Hummingbirds Sucking Nectar
Height: 17 cm (6.7 in) Diameter: 13 cm (5.1 in)

Pitcher Depicting a Pair of Sea Birds with Fish in Their Beaks
Height: 18 cm (6.9 in) Diameter: 18 cm (6.9 in)

Pitcher Depicting Two Birds in Profile
Height: 17 cm (6.7 in) Diameter: 14 cm (5.6 in)

Ceramic
Nazca (A.D. 1–700)
National Museum of Archaeology, Anthropology and History of Peru, Lima

For the Nazca, the most powerful sea creature was the killer whale. The image on the polychromed vessel above, far left, is thought to be a killer whale, depicted with humanoid arms, and the head and paws of a feline. The Nazca focus on the predator, symbolized in the killer whale, reflects an increase in warfare, as evidenced by the number of weapons and trophy heads found in Nazca burials.

(Top, left to right) Pitcher Depicting Hummingbirds Sucking Nectar
Height: 20 cm (7.9 in) Diameter: 17 cm (6.7 in)

Pitcher with a Representation of an Andean Deity
Height: 19 cm (7.5 in) Diameter: 15 cm (5.9 in)

Ceramic
Nazca (A.D. 1–700)
National Museum of Archaeology, Anthropology and History of Peru, Lima

Unlike the post-fire resin decoration characteristic of Paracas ceramics, a distinguishing feature of these and most Nazca ceramics is a polychrome slip-painted surface. Because slip paint is not as susceptible to extreme temperatures or moisture, Nazca ceramics have been better preserved than Paracas pottery.

(Center left) Pitcher Depicting a Female Supernatural Being
Height: 60 cm (23.6 in) Diameter: 14 cm (5.5 in)

(Center right) Pitcher Depicting Condors Devouring an Animal
Height: 18 cm (7.1 in) Diameter: 16 cm (6.3 in)

Ceramic
Nazca (A.D. 1–700)
National Museum of Archaeology, Anthropology and History of Peru, Lima

The headdress of the individual depicted on the vessel far left suggests a female figure. Fertility and abundance are symbolized by the presence of children at her feet.

(Bottom, left to right) Pitcher Depicting a Loche Squash
Height: 22 cm (8.7 in) Diameter: 18 cm (7.1 in)

Pitcher Depicting a Potato
Height: 17 cm (6.7 in) Diameter: 12 cm (4.7 in)

Paccha Depicting Pacae Fruit
Length: 37 cm (14.6 in) Diameter: 9 cm (3.5 in)

Ceramic
Chimú (A.D. 1100–1450)
National Museum of Archaeology, Anthropology and History of Peru, Lima

The paccha shown at left takes the shape of a native Peruvian fruit called pacae. *Under a thick layer of skin, these flattened pods contain rows of smooth black seeds in a sweet, juicy pulp. The loche squash is common on the northern coast of Peru. The potato was a gift to the world from ancient Peru.*

Chachapoyas culture made its home in the northern area, while the Inca placed a lowland outpost, Machu Picchu, on the eastern flank of the southern Andes.

The cultures of the Andes, while diverse due to disparate adaptive strategies, nevertheless shared the common challenge of survival in a region of interrelated environmental extremes. From a historical perspective, the end result of Andean cultural evolution can be said to be the successful integration of the various geographic zones. Yet while some early cultures dominated large areas, either by force or through religious influence, it would take the powerful machine of Inca administration to make the various adaptive strategies work within a single cultural system.

(Above, left to right) Pitcher in the Form of a Dog
Height: 17 cm (6.7 in) Diameter: 13 cm (5.1 in)

Ceramic
Sicán (Lambayeque) (A.D. 700–1370)
National Museum of Archaeology, Anthropology and History of Peru, Lima

Pitcher Depicting a Hairless Dog Clutching its Genitals
Height: 19 cm (7.5 in) Diameter: 17 cm (6.7 in)

Pitcher Depicting a Hairless Dog Suckling Her Pups
Height: 25 cm (9.8 in) Diameter: 16 cm (6.3 in)

Ceramic
Chimú (A.D. 1100–1450)
National Museum of Archaeology, Anthropology and History of Peru, Lima

Hairless dogs were bred by the coastal people of Peru. The vessels at far left and center depict dogs that have been scarred where cuts were made to collect sacrificial blood. The sculpted dog at far left wears the crown of the Andean lord Naymlap.

(Above, left to right) Pitcher in the Form of a Bird-Person Playing a Drum
Height: 29 cm (11.4 in) Diameter: 24 cm (9.4 in)

Whistling Pitcher in the Form of a Parrot
Height: 27 cm (10.6 in) Diameter: 21 cm (8.3 in)

Pitcher Depicting Sea Birds
Height: 20 cm (7.9 in) Diameter: 13 cm (5.1 in)

Pitcher in the Form of a Toucan
Height: 21 cm (8.3 in) Diameter: 22 cm (8.7 in)

Ceramic
Moche (A.D. 50–800)
National Museum of Archaeology, Anthropology and History of Peru, Lima

Stylized birds and other creatures with human limbs and features are common in Moche art, reflecting a belief in the connectedness between humans and animals.

(Opposite) Plate with Llamas and Decorative Motifs
Ceramic
Inca (A.D. 1200–1532)
Height: 5 cm (1.9 in) Diameter: 28 cm (10.9 in)
National Museum of Archaeology, Anthropology and
History of Peru, Lima

The polychrome motifs decorating this plate include
geometric designs, water and bird icons, and rows of
profiled llamas.

Pitcher in the Form of a Stylized Toad
Height: 22 cm (8.7 in) Diameter: 21 cm (8.3 in)

Pitcher with Relief Images of Sea Lions
Height: 19 cm (7.5 in) Diameter: 14 cm (5.5 in)

Ceramic Sculpture of a Sea Lion with a Sea Bird in Relief
Height: 12 cm (4.7 in) Diameter: 23 cm (9.1 in)

Pitcher Depicting a Mythical Sea Creature with a Feline Head
Height: 28 cm (11 in) Diameter: 40 cm (16 in)

Pitcher in the Form of a Sea Turtle
Height: 23 cm (9.1 in) Diameter: 24 cm (9.4 in)

Ceramic
Moche (A.D. 50–800)
National Museum of Archaeology, Anthropology and
History of Peru, Lima

(Above) Flared Bowl Depicting a Pool of Water
Ceramic
Moche (A.D. 50–800)
Height: 15 cm (5.9 in) Diameter: 14 cm (5.5 in)
National Museum of Archaeology, Anthropology and
History of Peru, Lima

*Two sculpted birds are perched on the rim of this bowl.
A chorus of toads lines the inside rim; the exterior is
decorated with anemones and starfish.*

Cup with Relief Image of the Moche God Aiapaec
Ceramic
Chancay (A.D. 1200–1450)
Height: 33 cm (12.6 in) Diameter: 24 cm (9.4 in)
National Museum of Archaeology, Anthropology
and History of Peru, Lima

*Moche artists often depicted Aiapaec as a face
surrounded by radiating crests of ocean waves. Here,
the artist may also have shaped Aiapaec in the image
of a starfish or octopus.*

(Opposite, top left) Pitcher in the Form of a Tuber
with Human and Animal Images
Height: 35 cm (13.8 in) Diameter: 27 (10.6 in)

*Animal and human images in the form of birds and
farmers' heads adorn this tuber-shaped vessel.*

(Opposite, top right) Bean-Shaped Pitcher with a
Human Face
Height: 19 cm (7.5 in) Diameter: 14 cm (5.5 in)

*This supernatural warrior is shown surrounded by
weapons, including a mace interlocked with a shield.
On the figure's forehead is a* tumi *(ceremonial axe),
which is thought to be a lunar symbol, and two
ornaments decorated with symbols of water drops.*

(Opposite, bottom left) Pitcher in the Form of a
Potato with Human and Feline Faces
Height: 25 cm (9.8 in) Diameter: 18 cm (7.1 in)

*This sculpted potato is depicted in a magical context.
Human faces with mutilated noses and lips replace
the potato's eyes.*

(Opposite, bottom right) Pitcher with a Mythical
Scene
Height: 24 cm (9.4 in) Diameter: 22 cm (8.7 in)

*This pitcher is composed of a compound chamber
with a mollusk-shaped top. The lower portion of the
vessel depicts a painted mythical scene with a cast of
serpents and mollusk gatherers.*

Ceramic
Moche (A.D. 50–800)
*National Museum of Archaeology, Anthropology and
History of Peru, Lima*

(Above) The badly eroded Sipán pyramids tower over sugar cane fields and a Moche burial platform. The taller of the two pyramids was raised by the Moche in A.D. 200, the smaller by another culture 500 years later. Periodic El Niño rains have contributed to the erosion of the pyramids.

(Opposite) A 15-foot-high icon of white granite portrays an eerie deity, half man, half jaguar. Called El Lanzón, it stands high in the Andes, embedded in dark local rock, at the heart of a temple complex called Chavín de Huántar. Artisans of the Chavín culture built the temple in around 850 B.C.

The Cultures of Ancient Peru

Complex, monument-building societies, sometimes called civilizations, go back at least four thousand years in Peru. The Andean people built large and complex cities, irrigated whole coastal valleys, worked with gold and other metals, wove textiles of intricate beauty, and made clay vessels so vivid that they seem more sculpture than pottery. They at times mummified their dead, but even more often the dry coastal sands of their burial places simply dried their bodies. They did not, however, develop a formal system of writing that we can read today, and most of what we know about them has been learned through a legacy of architectural remains, and the objects of stone, clay, gold, textiles, and other materials they buried with their dead. The Spanish reported on their experiences with the Inca during their conquest, another valuable source of information.

Archaeologists have built accurate chronologies of the cultures of pre-Columbian Peru, despite the destruction caused by looters who have taken countless artifacts—even mummies—from tombs or burial sites, and sold them with no record of where they originated. Researchers have studied artifacts and identified successive art styles in their effort to establish a cultural sequence for the various peoples of ancient Peru. In the last sixty years, more sites than ever before have been excavated by professional archaeologists, and these have been dated through scientific methods. For some cultures, we now understand a great deal about the people who produced the artifacts, their way of life, their political structures, and even some of their history. In other cases, however, we still know very little.

The area we now call Peru was probably never completely politically unified until the Inca conquest, which began in the 1400s. Yet through the thousands of years that people have lived in Peru, inter-regional exchange and evolving sociocultural complexity led to the spread of similar artifact styles over a large area. Scholars call the phenomenon of an art style that gains widespread popularity an archaeological horizon, a term used to judge approximate contemporaneity between distant sites. In the Central Andes of Peru, a series of major time periods has been organized around the

The Early Horizon site of Chavín de Huántar lies in a highland valley of the Mosna River at 10,000 feet in the north-central sierra. This early monumental site consists of platform mounds built in U-shaped arrangements around low square and circular plazas.

horizon concept. After an early period of hunting-gathering, known as the Preceramic Period, comes the Initial Period, which is marked by the first use of pottery. This is followed by five periods alternating between relatively widespread art styles (Early, Middle, and Late Horizons), and the intervening periods of stylistic differentiation (Early and Late Intermediate Periods). Late Horizon unity was caused by the extensive Inca Empire, and the Middle Horizon probably reflects smaller-scale states that were nevertheless quite large. The broad similarity of the Early Horizon cultures was most likely due to the adoption of religious cults by emerging elites in many parts of the Central Andes.

The following cultural sequence has been simplified, and includes only the best-known cultures, with emphasis on the coastal and highland regions.

First Cultures, 10,000–1000 B.C.

The earliest inhabitants of Peru arrived around 10,000 B.C. They were hunter-gatherers who used varied stone tool technologies to obtain resources from the diverse Andean environments. Over the next 7,000 years, they became increasingly specialized in the exploitation of regional resources,

and in some areas, such as the coast and highland valleys, small town-like communities became established. Substantial earth and rock platforms, among the earliest monumental architecture in the Americas, were built along the desert coast as early as 3000 B.C. By 2000 B.C., irrigation was in use for farming. As agriculture became more and more productive, the attraction of marine resources diminished, and settlements grew and moved deeper into the coastal valleys.

The coastal peoples were skilled at making fishing nets and other marine-oriented technology, and developed intricately decorated textiles. Like the nets, these textiles were often made by a process called twining, which produces a lace-like fabric. These very ancient textiles, some of which survive today, introduced many of the motifs that would play an ongoing role in the imagery of ancient Peru.

Important religious centers with monumental architecture were not the centers of large towns at this point, and most of the population was widely distributed in small communities. Early ceremonial centers were built with mounds along three sides of a large plaza, forming a U shape, with the open side facing the mountains, which were thought to

have religious significance. The life-giving rivers that fed the irrigation canals originated in the mountains; thus, the mountains, the water they brought, and perhaps fire became the foci of much religious activity.

Chavín, 1000–200 B.C.

In the first millennium B.C., a new architectural and artistic style spread across Peru. Similar deities and animal figures have been found on pottery and textiles throughout the country. These elements were brought together and most fully expressed at the site Chavín de Huántar. It is thought that Chavín was the center of a religious cult, and perhaps a source of some of the objects with Chavín iconography found across the Andes. Located in the headwaters of one of the large Amazon tributary rivers of the high Andes, Chavín could be reached from the coast only by crossing through the towering Andean ranges of the Cordilleras Negra and Blanca.

Chavín art is done in a complex and almost baroque style that combines central human figures with animal attributes, typically representing threatening body parts such as fangs, claws, or beaks. Many images were engraved around stone columns or shafts, making them difficult to read. Archaeologists believe that the Chavín style was intentionally difficult to interpret, and intended only for initiates of the cult.

At Chavín, the largest structure was the Castillo, a probable temple decorated with beautiful stone art, finely worked masonry, and built with remarkable engineering. At first glance, the monumental stone structure at Chavín de Huántar appears solid, but a number of stone-lined labyrinthine passages were

(Above, right) An anthropomorphic mural motif ornamenting the walls of Huaca del Sol, Pyramid of the Sun, located just east of Trujillo. It is thought that this pyramid served as the imperial palace and burial site for Moche heads of state.

(Right) Stone monolith in the Early Horizon site of Kuntur Wasi in the sierra of Cajamarca, northern Peru.

(Above) Huaca de la Luna—Pyramid of the Moon—in the Moche Valley, as seen from the top of Huaca del Sol. Huaca de la Luna houses the most expansive collection of Moche murals yet discovered.

(Left) Reconstruction of the Moche period mounds at the site of Sipán. One of the richest unlooted tombs of ancient Peru, impressive funerary offerings indicate the elite status of those buried here. The low platform in the lower left corner yielded the rich and renowned burial of the Lord of Sipán.

(Bottom left): This burial chamber in Tomb 2, a non-royal tomb, contained several human figures, as well as the skeleton of a headless llama, a reptile, and a dog. The animals may have been sacrificed as offerings or as food for the Moche in the afterworld.

(Opposite page): A golden necklace with human faces atop a spider-web motif accompanies the uncovered remains of the Old Lord of Sipán. Ceramic vessels, which may have contained offerings, flank the royal remains.

constructed in its interior, along with a maze of drains and vents. Water passing through some drains may have been used to create thunderous sounds in the chambers. The incised stones in Chavín's galleries depict magical-religious figures. The most common were jaguars, birds of prey, and reptiles, which were frequently anthropomorphized. These appear on the Raimondi Stone, a monolithic plaque that centers on the image of the Staff God, a central figure in the Chavín pantheon. With serpents for hair, fang-like canines, claws on hands and feet, and intricately carved vertical staffs in each hand, he is an impressive and imposing figure. Also from the Chavín site is the Tello Obelisk, a long, rectangular cross section stone shaft engraved with the image of a cayman, the south American alligator. The figure is depicted with manioc and other plants, indicating that it may have been associated with crops. Most impressive is the Lanzón monolith still lodged in the heart of the Old Temple, the form of which evokes an enormous knife. Called the "Snarling God," the figure also has snakes for hair and tusk-like canines in a mouth that seems to grimace or smile.

Chavín de Huántar must have been an early center of power in the context of the evolution of ancient Peruvian civilization. Many examples of objects with Chavín-like designs are scattered throughout the coastal and mountainous regions. When preservation conditions permit, Chavín designs are also found on textiles, which were light and easy to carry.

Important monuments related to Chavín de Huántar are Pacopampa and Kuntur Wasi, both located in the northern Peruvian sierra. In 1990, the tomb of a person of high status was discovered at Kuntur Wasi, accompanied by elaborate gold objects, crowns, and symbolic adornments. In the coastal Casma Valley, the site of Sechín Alto was occupied by 1400 BC. It contains the largest of all early monuments in the Americas in the form of a stone-faced platform mound 131 feet high, 984 feet long, and 820 feet wide. Artifacts uncovered at the nearby monument of Cerro Sechín bear stylistic similarities to those at Chavín. The walls of the temple are covered with images of dismembered figures and decapitated heads, interspersed between haughty warriors. While the scene may represent human sacrifice, it is perhaps more likely a depiction, or

(Above, left to right) Pitcher Depicting a Deformed Man
Height: 22 cm (8.9 in) Diameter: 18 cm (7.1 in)

Sculptural Pitcher Depicting a Seated Blind Man
Height: 32 cm (12.6 in) Diameter: 13 cm (5.1 in)

Pitcher in the Form of an Amputee
Height: 15 cm (6 in) Diameter: 10 cm (3.9 in)

Pitcher in the Form of a Potato with Mutilated Human Faces
Height: 20 cm (8.3 in) Diameter: 19 cm (7.9 in)

Pitcher Depicting a Deformed Man
Height: 24 cm (9.4 in) Diameter: 17 cm (6.7 in)

Ceramic
Moche (A.D. 50–800)
National Museum of Archaeology, Anthropology and
History of Peru, Lima

*The objects shown above depict individuals with serious
injuries or deformities—amputations, missing teeth,
blindness, and leishmaniasis, an insect-borne disease, which
attacks the soft tissues, especially the lips, nose, and ears.
While some of these injuries are the result of disease, others
were inflicted by humans as a form of punishment or, some
believe, for sacrificial purposes. Some Moche vessels, for
example, depict prisoners who bleed from the nose due to
cuts inflicted as a means of obtaining sacrificial blood.*

(Above) Woven Mantle with Human Images (detail)
Paracas (Necropolis) (700 B.C.–A.D. 1)
Width: 52 cm (20.3 in) Length: 61 cm (24.2 in)
National Museum of Archaeology, Anthropology and
History of Peru, Lima

*The cloak shown here has a central opening for the head, like
a poncho. Its design is composed of geometrically shaped
humans. Fringe runs on all sides.*

*(Opposite) The site of Karwa, to the south of the Paracas
Peninsula on the southern coast of Peru. Early Horizon
textiles from a Karwa tomb destroyed by looters show a
strong similarity to those of Chavín.*

even an exaggeration, of warfare between local or regional groups.

Paracas, 700 B.C.–A.D. 1

On the south coast, the archaeological site of Paracas gives its name to a group of people who lived in loosely affiliated farming and fishing villages. In a sector of the site called the Necropolis, more than 400 mummy bundles were buried in a tightly clustered pattern. Paracas Necropolis seems to have been the burial center for elite members of the society, with mummy bundles placed in either shaft tombs or in stone vaults. The bundles were made up of many layers of both plain and ornate textiles; ceramics and gold objects were found within and around them. The more elaborate textiles were of alpaca wool decorated with intricately embroidered polychrome figures. Some of these were made for burial while others were worn in life. Some crania of those buried at Paracas had been cut to remove wafer-size disks of bone, a form of trepanation. The exact reason for carrying out this procedure is not clear, but it may have served to remedy head wounds, relieve headaches, or may have had ritual importance. Smoothed edges on the bone near the excisions indicate regrowth and healing. In fact, some patients lived long after the surgery.

Early Paracas ceramics display imagery influenced by the Chavín style. Later pottery is painted with abstracted natural and supernatural images.

Nazca, A.D. 1–700

Eventually the Paracas culture transformed into the widespread south coast Nazca culture. The Nazca were apparently a loosely knit society with a fairly common ideology and religious affiliation. Nazca developed a highly refined ceramic style, characterized by beautifully painted polychrome vessels with extremely smooth surfaces. Stylized, abstract images of mythical beings, felines, foxes, and trophy heads are typical themes. In addition to their renowned pottery, Nazca is also known today for the so-called Nazca lines, a group of gigantic drawings of animals, trapezoid forms, and straight lines laid out on the arid desert. Called geoglyphs, they were created by removing the dark oxidized desert surface to reveal lower, lighter-colored sediments. Together these figures occupy a vast desert area between the modern town of Nazca and the Ingenio Valley to the north. The large images lie

(Above) Geoglyphs, or desert markings, for which the Nazca are particularly famous, occupy the pampa flats near the Rio Nazca. These ground drawings were created by brushing away the much darker surface desert sediment to expose the lighter shades of earth underneath.

on a flat desert surface that can only be viewed from the air, and were only discovered when flights started in this area. The figures evoke constellations, and might have represented something akin to a graphic calendar of gigantic proportions. According to some, like archaeologist Johan Reinhard, the motifs traced in the desert by the Nazca people were probably designed to encourage rain in the mountain ranges, which would nourish the rivers that fertilized the valleys of the coastal desert.

Moche, A.D. 50–800

The Moche, whose civilization was contemporaneous with the Nazca, resided on the north coast. Their political organizations, probably small and perhaps unstable states, were established through conflict and conquest. For these first states of the Andes, the Moche had capitals such as the site of Moche, not far from modern Trujillo. Gabled buildings and solid molded adobe brick platforms with ramps are characteristic of Moche architecture.

The Moche pioneered the use of press molds to produce large numbers of ceramic vessels, which circulated primarily among the upper classes of the society. Despite the fact that many basic forms were mass-produced, Moche ceramics reached a high level of artistic achievement in the finishing details of modeling and painting. Realistic portrayals of humans, animals, and plants are characteristic of Moche style. Their beautifully sculpted pottery speaks eloquently of warfare, ritual, sickness, and healing. They created individualized and expressive models of the natural, human, and supernatural

(Above) Pampa Grande was a large Moche complex of sacred rooms, ceremonial platforms, and living quarters that may have housed as many as 10,000 people. Its abrupt end is shrouded in mystery. The structures associated with the powerful elite seem to have been burned, after which the site was abandoned.

(Below) Entrance gateway to the heavily reconstructed Kalasasaya compound at Tiahuanaco, with a sunken court in the foreground.

(Opposite) Island of the Sun, Lake Titicaca. Islands in this high altitude lake lying between Peru and Bolivia were sacred to the Incas, who believed them to be the birthplaces of the sun and moon.

worlds. The aggressive, warlike nature of the Moche is reflected in the images of warriors and warfare depicted in ceramics, gold work, textiles and frescoes.

The Moche also depicted facets of their spiritual and material world on the walls of their more important buildings. Near the capital, the Moche built an enormous ceremonial complex, flanked by two large pyramidal complexes called Huaca del Sol and Huaca de la Luna. Here, colorful frescoes depict a fierce deity known today as the Decapitator God. The wealth of imagery in the various media have sometimes been taken as a broad record of the Moche world, but convincing arguments suggest that in fact the Moche were only portraying a very select group of objects and themes, perhaps derived from a pervasive mythology of the culture.

Huaca del Sol, or Pyramid of the Sun, is 131 feet high, 1,115 feet long, and 525 feet wide. It is estimated that more than 100 million sun-baked bricks were used in its construction. Large looting operations were conducted by the Spanish, and colonial documents indicate that great treasures were found here. This suggests that Huaca del Sol was a burial place for the elite, but the structure may have had a number of functions within the evolving large town of Moche. The smaller Huaca de la Luna, or Pyramid of the Moon, is distinguished by

(Above) Excavations in the Cheqo Wasi sector of the major Middle Horizon site of Huari, in the Ayacucho Valley of the south central sierra. Large cut-stone slabs form the walls of apparent tomb chambers, looted long ago.

(Opposite, top left) Pitcher Depicting Disembodied Supernatural Creatures and Symbols of Water
Ceramic
Tiahuanaco-Huari (A.D. 200–800)
Height: 15 cm (5.9 in) Diameter: 14 cm (5.5 in)
National Museum of Archaeology, Anthropology and History of Peru, Lima

(Opposite, top center) Pitcher Depicting Stylized Birds
Ceramic
Chincha (A.D. 1200–1450)
Height: 19 cm (7.5 in) Diameter: 14 cm (5.5 in)
National Museum of Archaeology, Anthropology and History of Peru, Lima

The pitchers opposite, top left, illustrate the use of textile patterns on ceramic vessels.

(Opposite, top right) Silver Mummy Mask
Tiahuanaco-Huari (A.D. 200–800)
Height: 14 cm (5.5 in) Diameter: 19 cm (7.4 in)
National Museum of Archaeology, Anthropology and History of Peru, Lima

Perforations on this mummy mask indicate that it was attached to the face of the deceased or to a funerary bundle.

(Opposite, center left) Pitcher Depicting the Lord Naymlap
Ceramic
Sicán (Lambayeque) (A.D. 700–1370)
Height: 24 cm (9.4 in) Diameter: 24 cm (9.4 in)
National Museum of Archaeology, Anthropology and History of Peru, Lima

Naymlap and two assistants in the form of monkeys watch as shamans perform ceremonies that have brought rain.

(Opposite, center right) Ceramic Incense Burner in the Form of a Feline
Tiahuanaco (A.D. 200–800)
Height: 26 cm (10.2 in) Diameter: 38 cm (15 in)
National Museum of Archaeology, Anthropology and History of Peru, Lima

(Opposite, bottom left) Silver Pitcher in the Form of a Lobster
Chimú (A.D. 1100–1450)
Height: 25 cm (9.8 in) Diameter: 22 cm (8.6 in)
National Museum of Archaeology, Anthropology and History of Peru, Lima

This piece is a silver copy of a ceramic vessel. The form of a monkey rests on the stirrup spout.

(Opposite, bottom right) Pitcher Depicting a Supernatural Being
Ceramic
Nazca (A.D. 1–700)
Height: 62 cm (24.4 in) Diameter: 47 cm (18.5 in)
National Museum of Archaeology, Anthropology and History of Peru, Lima

An anthropomorphic supernatural figure with symbolic attributes is depicted on this semi-sculpted vessel. The mustache, composed of two stylized birds, is suggestive of feline whiskers.

its wall murals, which show a variety of painted figures in low relief. Some of these seem to represent deities associated with human decapitation, and other evidence seems to indicate that this religious center witnessed elaborate rituals perhaps involving human sacrifice.

Just north of Moche, on the Chicama Valley coast, stands the Moche archaeological complex of El Brujo. A major platform there, Huaca Cao Viejo, measuring 426 by 558 feet, was also decorated with colorful murals. The principle, tiered facade was decorated with polychrome friezes of typical Moche ritual iconography. There are warriors engaged in hand-to-hand combat, prisoners stripped of their clothes with ropes around their necks, and finally the sacrifice of these captives by the Decapitator God. As with Huaca de la Luna, it now seems probable that the friezes depict rituals actually carried out at the site.

Well to the north, in the valley of Lambayeque, is Sipán, where Peru's richest unlooted tombs were discovered and excavated by archaeologist Walter Alva. The pyramid at Sipán was not the burial place of a single Moche lord, rather it was a necropolis containing what may be interpreted as a whole lineage of leaders. At least three tombs remained intact when Alva began his excavations. There he found superb objects of Moche gold unsurpassed in detail and workmanship. Many of the individuals buried with this wealth were probably key actors in the types of rituals portrayed at El Brujo and Moche.

Tiahuanaco, A.D. 200–800, and Huari, A.D. 650–800

The Huari were an aggressive people who probably conquered the Nazca and built an empire that may have covered much of present-day Peru. They originated in the southern highlands, and gained dominance of the south-central Peruvian coast between A.D. 500 and 650. It is possible that Huari could have expanded rapidly in the Andes as a result of environmental problems affecting other cultures that the Huari were better prepared to survive. Some of these advantages may have

(Above) A tomb looter, or huaquero, digging in a cemetery of coastal Peru. The international market for prehistoric art underwrites this devastating destruction of Peru's archaeological patrimony. (Opposite) This pre-Inca cemetery near Lima has been desecrated by huaqueros. Tombs have been plundered for gold and other treasures at least since the Spanish conquistadors. There is evidence that even the Incas pillaged the burial sites and temples of their ancestors in search of riches and building materials.

stemmed from more effective and drought-tolerant agricultural practices.

Near the present-day city of Ayacucho stands what is considered to have been the capital of the Huari empire. This massive center of administrative, residential, and religious architecture included complex multistoried buildings enclosed by high walls. The settlement was originally surrounded by an extensive irrigation system. The compartmentalization of the city into large rectangular compounds suggests an architectural emphasis on the segregation of classes or other social units. One enclosure, the Cheqo-Wasi, contained funerary chambers constructed of finely worked stone. Although looted in antiquity, these may have been the tombs of Huari monarchs.

By the same time that the Huari conquered the southern coastal region, a related kingdom, called Tiahuanaco, had already grown up around Lake Titicaca in Bolivia, just south of modern-day Peru. The two cultures seem to have a number of common stylistic features, and may have shared some cultural ancestry. Evidence suggests that while the Huari culture achieved dominance through conquest and the building of an empire, Tiahuanaco may have been more of a religious and trade-oriented center. While there is little evidence of Tiahuanaco architecture in the regions dominated by Huari structures, Tiahuanaco pottery, textiles, and metalwork are found throughout a large region.

Nine miles southeast of Lake Titicaca, however, stand the world-famous ruins of Tiahuanaco proper, dominated by a massive pyramid known as Akapana, and by the Kalasasaya, a heavily reconstructed compound and colossal gateway. Perhaps the most impressive architectural features at Tiahuanaco are the portals, each rendered from a single block of stone. The most elaborate of these is the Gateway of the Sun, dominated by a central character somewhat reminiscent of the Chavín Staff God. He wears an elaborate headdress, decorative necklace, tunic, and kilt, and hold staffs terminating in condor heads.

Some of the style and iconography of Tiahuanaco-Huari was also present in Pachacamac, on the outskirts of Lima, where an important religious center was developing. In Pachacamac, a distinctive type of Tiahuanaco-Huari ceramic originated, and is known as the Pachacamac style. The Incas, respectful of the ancient prestige of the sanctuary of Pachacamac, later erected new buildings at the site to exert their own influence on a cult they could not easily suppress.

Sicán (Lambayeque), A.D. 700–1370

Toward the end of the Huari period, a regional style emerged in the north coastal valleys, centered around the Lambayeque valley. Only recently have serious investigations begun on the culture that invented the style, but these valleys were incorporated into the Chimú empire around the 1300s.

The Lambayeque style is identified by ceramics formed in elaborate molds. As with all of the north coast styles after the Moche, the two-part mold continued to be used, but the vessels lacked the high level of artistry achieved by the Moche. Whistling pots and double-spouted bottles bearing the images of individuals with elaborate headdresses are characteristic of the style. Batán Grande, an

Burial towers at the Late Intermediate Period site of Sillustani, in the southern altiplano near Lake Titicaca.

enormous complex of both monumental and domestic buildings near Chiclayo, was the apparent center of Lambayeque culture. There was an architectural emphasis on truncated pyramids, large platforms with ramps, colonnades, chamber and fill construction, and the use of adobes. The Huacas La Ventana and Loro of Batán Grande, among others, were apparently the locations of numerous looting forays that produced objects of gold of great value. Near Batán Grande, is the massive Lambayeque architectural complex of Túcume. Long platforms and truncated pyramids surround a pointed natural hill, a site also occupied by the Chimú and the Inca.

Chancay, A.D. 1200–1450

After the fall of the Huari empire, a style called Chancay arose in the central coast along several river valleys. This culture is known from its ceramics, and especially a fine talent for textile weaving. The Chancay may have fallen under the influence of the Chimú around 1400. Chancay potters are most noted for producing human effigy vessels that were first coated with a white slip, then decorated with a dark brown inky paint.

Chimú A.D. 1100–1450

The capital of the Chimú empire, Chan Chán, was located only a few miles from the old Moche center of Huaca del Sol and Huaca de la Luna. The Chimú forged an empire along the north coast that was large enough to keep the Incas at bay for some time. They constructed enormous cities of adobe decorated with frescoes and carvings in the mud walls. Chimú ceramics did not have the artistry of the earlier Nazca or Moche vessels, but the Chimú were master metalsmiths, producing beautiful objects of gold and silver.

The metropolis of Chan Chán, the world's most extensive adobe city, lies on the outskirts of Trujillo. Its central area is divided into approximately ten walled rectangular compounds, each containing houses, terraces, reservoirs, gardens, and low burial mounds. When a lord died in Chan Chán, his palace was converted into a mortuary estate, from which his descendants continued to gather tribute and exert influence. This custom was followed by Inca lords in Cuzco, who did not inherit the estates of their predecessors, but instead had to forge a new segment of the empire in order to supply their own resources.

Empire of the Incas

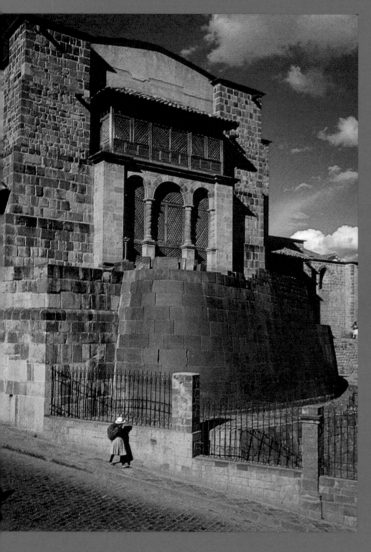

Prior to their emergence as the conquerors of a vast empire, the Incas were a small and politically unimportant group residing in the southern Peruvian highlands. Around A.D. 1400, they began their expansion through conquest, combining formidable warfare tactics with highly efficient organization, enabling them to maintain extremely tight control over a far-flung empire.

The Incas claimed to have descended from Inti, the Sun God, perhaps the most important god in their pantheon. About twelve kings were recorded who had descended from the original children of Inti, Manco Capac and Mama Ocllo, a brother and sister who married and founded the line. According to Inca beliefs, Cuzco was chosen as the capital and center of the world when the golden staff they carried sank into the earth at that spot. The Incas believed that civilization and enlightenment originated in Cuzco, around which the world was divided into four quarters; the realm of the Incas was called Tahuantinsuyu, the Land of the Four Quarters. From Cuzco emerged four great state roads leading into the regions of Chinchaysuyo, Collasuyo, Contisuyo, and Antisuyo. These roads, added to alternate roads and those joining the principal highways, extended for 20,000 miles. Suspension bridges hundreds of feet long allowed passage over deep gorges. The Inca emperors created a state with a territory extending nearly 3,000 miles whose government and administration were highly effective and efficient. The empire had a carefully planned economic structure, which developed and employed agricultural techniques appropriate to the often hostile environment.

(Left) In the center of Cuzco, the walls of the most sacred Inca shrine, the Temple of the Sun, now support a Dominican church, founded in 1534. This sacred wall of the Coricancha, or "golden enclosure," was constructed without mortar, yet has withstood centuries of natural disasters, while the Spanish church has been rebuilt several times. At the height of the Inca Empire, its walls were covered in sheaths of gold, which were stripped by the Spanish conquerors.

(Opposite) This stone-paved Inca road leads into Machu Picchu. Although not as wide as many Inca imperial roads, it too was elaborately engineered.

(Top left) Manco Capac, Mythical Father of the Incas

(Top right) Mama Ocllo, Mythical Mother of the Incas

Colonial Period (ca. 1850)
Oil on Canvas
Dimensions: .9 x .75 m (36 x 40 in)
National Museum of Archaeology, Anthropology and
History of Peru, Lima

*These colonial-era portraits depict Mama Ocllo and her
husband-brother, Manco Capac. According to Inca
mythology, they were the offspring of the Sun God Inti, and
together they founded the Inca dynasty.*

(Below) Enameled Wooden Cups (Queros)
Inca/Colonial (ca. 1600s)
Height: 17 cm (6.7 in) Diameter: 14 cm (5.5 in)
Banco de Crédito del Perú

These ceremonial cups, or queros, *are sculpted from wood.
Cavities carved into the wood are filled with a colorful resin.
On the quero below left, a human couple of high rank are
shown under a rainbow. Parrots and other animals are
rendered realistically on the cup below right.*

Cuzco: Sacred City

Cuzco was expanded in 1438 by the great Inca
emperor Pachacuti, or Earthshaker. Early in his
career, Pachacuti had defended Cuzco against a
powerful enemy, and subsequently launched many
successful expansion campaigns. He then turned
toward organizing and consolidating the vast Inca
gains. Leaving the imperial troops to his son, Topa
Inca, who had also become an excellent tactician,
expanding the Inca empire into Ecuador and central
Chile, Pachacuti returned to Cuzco. There he created
or upgraded institutions such as the highway and
communications systems, an expansive warehousing
system, and a system of national taxation.

As a young man, Pachacuti had seen Inti, the
Sun God, in a vision. This provided the inspiration
for his considerable accomplishments. He chose to
honor Inti by enlarging and embellishing Cuzco,
the administrative and religious capital of the Inca
empire. Royal rooms were built around the
enormous dual plaza of Haucaypata-Cusipata, part
of which still functions as the central plaza of
Cuzco. He commissioned Cuzco's most important
sanctuary, the Coricancha, a marvelous
construction believed to have been the Temple of
the Sun. Early chroniclers claim that in the
Coricancha were life-size gold replicas of plants,
birds, and llamas, and a golden figure of the sun
decked in precious jewels. Also within the
Coricancha were the mummified bodies of
emperors, dressed in fine clothes and
accompanied by sumptuous and emblematic
jewelry. Among the other treasures found there
were shimmering sheets of gold that covered the
doorways and walls. These precious metal objects
were looted by the Spanish conquerors, and
melted down as plunder.

(Above) Detail of the walls of Sacsahuaman, a massive Inca stone construction on a hill overlooking Cuzco. Historically, the site served as a fortress, but may have had a variety of functions, including ritual.

(Right) Pitcher with Geometric Motifs
Height: 33 cm (13 in) Diameter: 29 cm (11.3 in)

(Far right) Paccha with Geometric Motifs and the Head of a Rodent
Height: 19 cm (7.4 in) Diameter: 15 cm (5.9 in)

Ceramic
Inca (A.D. 1200–1532)
National Museum of Archaeology, Anthropology and History of Peru, Lima

Geometric motifs adorn these polychrome Aribalo vessels.

(Above) The so-called Intihuatana sector of the Inca estate of Pisac, above the Vilcanota Valley, shows imperial-style cut-stone architecture at its finest, and demonstrates the Inca talent for setting architecture into the landscape. A royal retreat near Cuzco, Pisac was commissioned by Inca Emperor Pachacuti. Made of red volcanic stone with coursed masonry, its design suggests that it functioned as both a fortress and an imperial residence.

Economic Administration of the Inca Empire

Labor to build public works, like the extensive road network, was assembled through an obligatory system of labor, called *mita*. Mita, literally "a turn," was essentially a period of time in labor owed to the government. The service personnel of the mita rotated through this labor taxation, spending their time building and repairing roads, mining precious metals, or serving in the army.

Another government-managed organization was the *acllacuna*, made up of women chosen for a life of religious devotion, elite craft production, or for serving as concubines to noble Inca. The *Acllahuasi*, House of Chosen Women, was in the main square near the Coricancha, indicating its importance in Inca society. The *acllas* were chosen at around age ten on the basis of skill and beauty. They were taught and perfected many skills, such as weaving and the making of *chicha* (a corn-based alcoholic beverage used in rituals). From them the emperor chose wives for himself, and some were given as rewards to nobles. Others served as priestesses, known as virgins of the sun. Chastity was the absolute rule. Violation meant death for both parties. Unlike mita, the labor tribute of the acllas was rendered for life. Another form of tribute to the government was in goods, particularly foodstuffs. The state saw that each family received a determined quantity of land to cultivate, from which it demanded two-thirds of the production. The government used this surplus in part to support the general administration and religious leaders. Part of it, however, was accumulated in silos for other state purposes, including the feeding of the army. Some believe that the Incas may have provided for those in need from these stores, but it is likely that little went to serve the general population. To preserve their stored reserves, the Incas turned to a variety of food preservation techniques. Meat, for example, was dehydrated into *charqui* (now known in English as jerky, derived from the Inca word) and potatoes were freeze dried.

To more efficiently exercise their dominion over and administrate their subjects, the Incas organized the general population into units of 10, 100, 1,000,

(Above) The high terraces and elaborate Inca cut-stone structures of Ollantaytambo were still in construction at the time of the Spanish arrival. They would likely have been part of a royal facility, as reflected in their grandiose design.

or 10,000 taxpaying units (often families), perhaps further subdivided into groupings of 50, 500, and 5,000. A whole hierarchy of administrators was charged with specific groups within this scheme. Divisions were also made according to age, through which the productivity of each person was determined. From childhood, individuals were required to comply with the obligations appropriate to their age.

In order to achieve satisfactory harvests, the Incas often engaged in ritual procedures that were intended to sway the will of supernatural powers. To gain the approval of the gods, it was necessary to offer sacrifices of all kinds, from sea shells to llama fetuses, and, in some cases, humans. The Incas also perfected the construction and use of terraces for cultivation. This system expanded the agrarian frontier by making abrupt mountain slopes productive, and, at the same time, preventing erosion. Agriculture in the coastal valleys was also

expanded by building canals that improved and extended the major hydraulic works of earlier cultures. Some of the canal systems inherited by the Incas carried water dozens of miles, involving considerable engineering expertise.

Long-distance communication was established by way of messages carried by runners. The transmission of urgent messages across Inca territory was achieved by *chasqui*, or individual runners, spread out along the royal roads at distances that could be covered quickly by one person. Messages were relayed from runner to runner until the news arrived at its final destination. The messages may have been verbal, but also might have been recorded in knot records called *quipus*. The Incas were able to keep accurate census and accounting records using quipus, a system of knotted strings radiating from a base cord. Numerical data could be recorded using different types and positions of knots on strings of varying

length and color. Those trained to make and read quipus were known as the *quipucamayoc*; some believe they also recorded historical information.

The Ruler, the Nobility, and the Commoners

Society in the Inca empire was divided into nobility and various lower classes. Apart from those who distinguished themselves in war or other state activities, it was rare to change social status. It is for this reason that William Prescott wrote, referring to the individual in the Inca empire, "as he was born, so shall he die." Myths, like that of Viracocha, the Creator, imparted to the population the belief that nobles and commoners were born unequal by divine designation. Viracocha was said to have gone to Tiahuanaco, where he modeled people and animals from the primordial clay that he gathered there. He then painted on the people the various costumes that would forever distinguish their ethnicity and class. The Incas used this kind of ideology to maintain a strict social hierarchy. Internal disputes did exist in the form of rivalries

(Above) The elaborate cut-stone architecture of the Inca sub-capital of Huanuco Pampa sits on a high plain in the central sierra. In the foreground is a fountain with dual water channels leading to it. (Below) The Inca-Spanish chronicler Felipe Guamán Poma de Ayala's sketch of an Inca clerk with a quipu made of cotton or wool cord and string. Lacking a written language, Inca administrators used quipus to record everything necessary to run the empire.

over dynastic succession within the nobility. The Inca ruler was at the apex of the nobility. Next were his closest relatives, followed by the members of Cuzco's nobility and the nobility of the annexed provinces. The remaining population was composed primarily of common farmers. The *yanacona* were a group of servants or retainers whose status depended on many factors, including their own origin and the status of the individuals they served.

Inca nobility dressed in clothes made of cotton and alpaca wool, and wore sandals and sumptuous earrings. The Inca emperor, or Sapa Inca, wore a highly symbolic headdress consisting of a fringed cord that wrapped around his head. The emperor also carried symbolic staffs, and was transported on a litter with great pomp. All of this ostentation served to emphasize his power and assure that his orders were followed. The dress of ordinary Incas was not entirely different in style from that of the governors and nobles. Differences were found mainly in the quality of the workmanship displayed, and in the degree of decoration of the fabric, which for the average Inca was much more simple and rustic. Marriage customs varied in different parts of the empire, and probably also across social statuses. Adulterers were punished severely, sometimes with death. The punishments applied for infractions varied

according to social status. Commoners did not seek personal wealth, since money was unknown to them and precious metals did not constitute commercial means. Precious metals belonged to the state, and were used in ritual decoration and in royal insignia.

The Incas believed that in death the nobility maintained the same socio-economic status in the afterlife as they had enjoyed in life. Those in power continued ruling in the afterlife, surrounded by concubines and enjoying privileges. Inca nobility were mummified, and a court was maintained for them with an elaborate array of precious artifacts. The Inca system provided enormous privileges to the

(Below left) Quipu
Width: 43 cm (16.8 in) Length: 55 cm (21.8 in)

Using colored strings and knots, the Incas recorded numeric and other information on quipus. The position or color of the knots and strings represented complex messages read only by trained quipucamayoc *(quipu keepers).*

(Below) Woven Textile Fragment with Images of Llamas and People
Width: 147 cm (57.7 in) Length: 130 cm (51.1 in)

Inca (A.D. 1200–1532)
National Museum of Archaeology, Anthropology and History of Peru, Lima

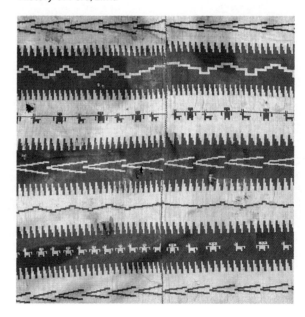

(Above, left to right) Paccha in the Form of a Feline
Height: 10 cm (3.9 in) Diameter: 16 cm (6.3 in)

Pitcher Depicting a Bird
Height: 18 cm (7 in) Diameter: 12 cm (4.7 in)

Bowl in the Form of Two Felines Attacking a Llama
Height: 10 cm (3.9 in) Diameter: 15 cm (5.9 in)

Paccha in the Form of a Coiled Serpent
Height: 17 cm (6.7 in) Diameter: 10 cm (3.9 in)

Paccha in the Form of the Head of a Feline
Height: 15 cm (5.9 in) Diameter: 11 cm (4.3 in)

Inca (A.D. 1200–1532)
National Museum of Archaeology, Anthropology
and History of Peru, Lima

The objects shown above may have been used in
rain or fertility rituals. Several are pacchas,
identified by the spout at the bottom of the vessel.

(Left and below left) Carved and Polished
Figures of Alpacas
Volcanic rock
Inca (A.D. 1200–1532)
Height: 7 cm (2.8 in) Diameter: 10 cm (3.9 in)
National Museum of Archaeology, Anthropology
and History of Peru, Lima

The polished alpaca sculptures shown here are
made from volcanic rock. Such objects, known as
ullti, were used in livestock fertility rites. Residue
from the fat of South American camelids was
found in the cavity in the back of the object.

(Above) A view beneath Machu Picchu's Temple of the Sun. This natural fissure was considered a huaca, *or holy object, by the Incas.*

governing Inca and his family. But it also allowed its commoners, the great majority of the population, to provide themselves with the basic needs of life. The responsibility of supply fell upon the shoulders of local governors or *curaca*, who were conscious of this and strove to satisfactorily fulfill their obligation. Propagandistic actions, initiated by the elite and diffused by the state, contributed to a feeling of state solidarity. This seems to have led to a type of conformism in which there were perhaps few aspirations for upward social movement, social change, or the accumulation of wealth.

Art and Architecture

The Inca empire inherited a rich and ancient tradition of artistic expression. This is reflected in their exquisite ceramics, textiles, and metallurgy. Their most significant and original contribution, however, was in architecture and engineering, which resulted in the building of masterful administrative and religious monuments, as well as in the construction and maintenance of an immense network of roads and irrigation works.

The city of Machu Picchu is an exceptional testament to the high level of achievement reached by Inca architecture. The site is located on a mountain ridge covered by exuberant Amazon flora, on the eastern descent from Cuzco toward the tropical lowlands. The grandeur of the landscape surrounding Machu Picchu heightens the beauty of its temples, shrines, patios, and staircases. Many parts of the site are built of hand-cut stones, which fit together so perfectly that even today, a knife cannot be inserted between the stones.

After the fall of the Inca empire, Machu Picchu stood abandoned and forgotten for nearly 500 years. Then, in 1911, this Inca architectural jewel was discovered by Hiram Bingham, a professor of Latin American History at Yale University. Bingham was intent on finding the lost city of Vilcabamba, the

final ruling place of the Incas after the Spanish took Cuzco. He believed it to be hidden in the densely forested valley near the Urubamba River. A trail newly blasted by the Peruvian government allowed Bingham to follow a little-known stretch of the river. Informed by a local farmer that there were Inca ruins higher up, he set off on the morning of July 24, 1911, with the farmer and one other companion. Climbing a steeply terraced hillside dating from Inca times, he came upon a magnificent find. Although partly covered by the trees, moss, and tangled vines that had grown over the site for centuries, he found, among other buildings, finely built temples, burial caves, and dwellings for the elite made of white granite, perfectly fitted together without the use of mortar. The site was intricately terraced; the whole city looked as if it had been carved out of the mountain. Bingham came to believe that this was indeed Vilcabamba. It wasn't until 1964 that Gene

Savoy, another American explorer, found the true final refuge of the Incas, in a much more remote location at still lower altitudes.

The Fall of the Inca Empire

At the time of the Spanish arrival to the Andes, the Inca empire covered an immense territory that surpassed the borders of modern day Peru. It included Ecuador, parts of Colombia and Bolivia, northwestern Argentina, and northern Chile. It is remarkable that the Spanish were able to conquer this highly organized, successful, and warlike empire of perhaps ten million subjects with only a few hundred men, some riding horses and a few armed with guns. The Spanish were able to do so in part because the Land of the Four Quarters had already fallen victim to the plague of smallpox. Brought by Europeans, the disease traveled swiftly through the population of the New World, far ahead of actual contact with the Spanish. Not only was the Inca

(Top) A stairway in front of the Palace of the Princess leads to the so-called Temple of the Sun, named by its discoverer, Hiram Bingham, who thought its curved walls reminiscent of the Temple of the Sun in Cuzco.

(Left) A photo of Hiram Bingham taken during the famous 1911 exhibition that led him to discover Machu Picchu.

(Opposite) The famous site of Machu Picchu is now known to have formed part of an Inca royal estate. Not the "lost capital of the Incas," as Hiram Bingham thought, it may have begun as a military outpost as the Incas expanded east from Cuzco.

(Above) This granite slab, located in front of the Temple of Three Windows at Machu Picchu, may have served as sacrificial stone. (Opposite) A photo taken by Hiram Bingham during the 1911 expedition. On the summit of a spectacular precipice, the Incas constructed a signal station from which the city below could be alerted to the approach of an enemy.

empire suffering from the devastating effects of the disease, which decimated the population, it was also torn apart by civil war, in part a result of the tumult created by the plague. While the Spanish were exploring the Pacific Coast in 1527, the Inca emperor Wayna Capac died. Two of his sons, Huascar and Atahualpa, then began a series of disputes over who would inherit power, leading to civil war. By manipulating this situation, and through other deceitful means, the Spanish were able to gain a foothold in Tahuantinsuyu. Atahualpa might have conceived of gaining the Spaniards' support for his cause, while some communities, harshly governed by the Incas, believed they had much to gain by escaping Inca rule. For this reason, many Andean cultures received the "strange bearded men" with special favor.

The decisive encounter between the Spanish and the Incas ended in massacre and the capture of Atahualpa, who as a prisoner promised to pay his ransom in objects of gold and silver. While amassing the promised quantity, he was accused by the conquerors of trumped-up crimes. In a sham

proceeding, Atahualpa was sentenced to die, and murdered on June 26, 1532. Seen from the native perspective, this appalling history and the suffering experienced by Andean cultures can be described in one suggestive Inca phrase: *chaupi punzhapi tutayarca*—"out of daylight came darkness."

Of course, it was the Spaniards' search for gold that brought them to the land of the Incas. Here they found gold beyond their wildest dreams: temple walls covered with gold, gold doors, gold vessels. In the years following the conquest, looting operations became so large, they were synonymous with mining. Pre-Inca tomb sites and monuments were divided into claim areas, and title holders established corporations to enlist the immense work force necessary to systematically excavate them. The reports of the conquistadors tell us that the Incas made dazzling sculpture and decorations using the precious metal. Little is left for us to see today, because the Spanish melted the gold into bars, which were easier to ship back to Spain. Today, it is primarily through their amazing architecture that we see the genius of the Incas.

The Human World

The environment of Peru played a decisive role in the development of Andean civilization. Andean people responded to the often hostile conditions by devising methods, such as irrigation, fertilization, terracing of mountain slopes, and the excavation of sunken gardens down to the water table, that made their surroundings manageable and even productive. Andean spirituality was also strongly influenced by nature and the environment. Ancient Peruvians believed in various gods of land and water. Some gods of water are fierce, emphasized by the presence of large tusk-like fangs, such as those depicted in representations of Aiapaec. Aiapaec was a demonic god, as capricious as El Niño, who tormented humanity with his power over the climate. To pacify him, the Andeans continually made offerings and sacrifices. Andean deities did not preside over a moral order, but were deemed

(Above, left) Pitcher in the Form of a Robed Man
Ceramic
Tiahuanaco-Huari (A.D. 200–800)
Height: 50 cm (19.5 in) Diameter: 33 cm (12.9 in)
National Museum of Archaeology, Anthropology and History of Peru, Lima

This ceramic vessel is similar to stone sculptures found at Huacaurara (Ayacucho) in Peru. The turban and face are covered with symbols of stepped agricultural terraces.

(Opposite) Stone Sculpture of a Standing Figure
Pukara (200 B.C. –A.D. 200)
Height: 43 cm (16.8 in) Diameter: 16 cm (6.4 in)
National Museum of Archaeology, Anthropology and History of Peru, Lima

This stone figure, depicted standing on a pedestal with hands and arms on his chest, wears a huara or loincloth.

(Above, left to right) Vase Depicting a Severed Head
Height: 19 cm (7.4 in) Diameter: 12 cm (4.7 in)

Bowl Depicting a Severed Head
Height: 10 cm (3.9 in) Diameter: 11 cm (4.2 in)

Pitcher in the Form of a Decapitated Head
Height: 16 cm (6.3 in) Diameter: 22 cm (8.6 in)

Ceramic
Nazca (A.D. 1–700)
National Museum of Archaeology, Anthropology and
History of Peru, Lima

*These vessels take the form of trophy heads, which were
often placed in Nazca burials. It was the Nazca custom, as
shown above, to fasten the lips together with thorns.*

(Far left) Vase Depicting Standing Figures
Height: 20 cm (7.8 in) Diameter: 11 cm (4.3 in)

(Left) Vase Depicting Dancing Figures
Height: 25 cm (9.8 in) Diameter: 14 cm (5.5 in)

Ceramic
Nazca (A.D. 1–700)
National Museum of Archaeology, Anthropology and
History of Peru, Lima

*The figures on these vessels carry arrows or spears, and wear
feathered headdresses. They are depicted with beaks and
have three fingers and toes on each hand, suggesting birds.
The faces on their loincloths represent severed heads.*

The Human World

rather to be in control of all things related to subsistence, including nature. The establishment of a moral order and the punishment of offenders were concerns of humans, particularly those living under developed governments.

The most common language of Peru at the time of the conquest was dubbed Quechua by the Spanish, a term they had used for a region of the sierras, and by extension, for the people who lived there. The original name of the Inca language was *Runa Simi* (literally, "man-mouth"), a version of which was imposed as the official language of the empire. Quechua is still spoken by millions in the Andes. Other languages that survived the conquest include *Mochica*, which was spoken along the northern coast until the end of the nineteenth century, and *Aymara*, which is still spoken in the Peruvian-Bolivian highlands.

Warfare

Warring among the different cultures of ancient Peru was one consequence of rapid population growth

(Below, left to right) Portrait Pitcher in the Form of a Common Man
Height: 17 cm (6.6 in) Diameter: 10 cm (3.8 in)

Pitcher Depicting a Common Person
Height: 24 cm (9.4 in) Diameter: 20 cm (7.8 in)

Pitcher in the Form of a Seated Man with a Swollen Face
Height: 26 cm (10.1 in) Diameter: 18 cm (7 in)

Pitcher Depicting a Wrinkled Woman
Height: 21 cm (8.2 in) Diameter: 18 cm (7 in)

Pitcher Depicting a Common Man
Height: 23 cm (9 in) Diameter: 20 cm (7.8 in)

Ceramic
Moche (A.D. 50–800)
National Museum of Archaeology, Anthropology and History of Peru, Lima

While most portrait vessels depict high-ranking individuals, these represent the common man. The wrinkles on the woman display extensive detail, which is typical of the realism in Moche art.

and the economic problems that resulted from it. The region had limited arable land, a situation made worse by devastating climatic events. The Inca-Spanish chronicler Felipe Guamán Poma de Ayala, who wrote his *New Chronicle and Good Government* around 1600 (a nearly 1,200-page letter to King Philip III detailing Inca life and protesting the negative effects of Spanish rule), said that the principal cause of warmongering, prior to the Inca era, was the lack of arable land in Peru, where there were "people who multiplied like ants."

There is much ancient iconographic representation of war, especially in the pictorial repertoire of Moche ceramics. The warriors and their clothing are illustrated in these ceramics, along with armor, war emblems, and weapons. Maces, lances, sling shots, and small square shields were the weapons of choice among the Moche. Curiously, in the middle of the Moche period some 1,500 years ago, Andeans rarely employed the bow and arrow.

Through their authoritarian system of labor taxation, the Incas were able to field armies of tens

(Above, left to right) Portrait Pitcher in the Form of a Man of High Status
Height: 28 cm (10.9 in) Diameter: 16 cm (6.2 in)

Portrait Pitcher
Height: 31 cm (12.1 in) Diameter: 18 cm (7 in)

Portrait Pitcher in the Form of a Man Wearing a Ceremonial Headdress
Height: 21 cm (8.2 in) Diameter: 15 cm (5.9 in)

Portrait Pitcher in the Form of a Man of Middle Status
Height: 26 cm (10.1 in) Diameter: 20 cm (7.8 in)

Pitcher in the Form of a Smiling Face
Height: 14 cm (5.7 in) Diameter: 16 cm (6.4 in)

Ceramic
Moche (A.D. 50–800)
National Museum of Archaeology, Anthropology and History of Peru, Lima

Most of the above stirrup-spout vessels depict high-ranking individuals, as indicated by the cloth turbans they wear.

(Above, left to right) Bowl with Images of Severed Heads
Height: 7 cm (2.8 in) Diameter: 18 cm (7 in)

Bowl Depicting the Head of a Mythical Being
Height: 16 cm (6.3 in) Diameter: 23 cm (9 in)

Bowl Depicting the Head of a Mythical Being
Height: 20 cm (7.8 in) Diameter: 18 cm (7 in)

Ceramic
Nazca (A.D. 1–700)
National Museum of Archaeology, Anthropology and
History of Peru, Lima

(Right) Pitcher Depicting a Female Healer
Moche (A.D. 50–800)
Height: 22 cm (8.6 in) Diameter: 17 cm (6.6 in)
National Museum of Archaeology, Anthropology and
History of Peru, Lima

*This female healer is represented in an attitude of prayer or
trance, eyes closed, grasping a bundle of medicinal plants.*

(Above, left to right) Pitcher in the Form of a Kneeling Warrior
Height: 23 cm (9 in) Diameter: 18 cm (7 in)

Pitcher in the Form of a Warrior
Height: 18 cm (7 in) Diameter: 15 cm (5.9 in)

Pitcher in the Form of a Seated Man
Height: 21 cm (8.2 in) Diameter: 20 cm (7.8 in)

Ceramic
Moche (A.D. 50–800)
National Museum of Archaeology, Anthropology and History of Peru, Lima

The figure above, far right, wears the classic Moche turban fastened to the chin, along with enormous earrings. The two figures above left and center depict Moche warriors.

(Below left) Pitcher in the Form of a Human Figure in a Robe
Height: 24 cm (9.4 in) Diameter: 19 cm (7.4 in)

(Below right) Pitcher with Three Decorative Bands
Height: 21 cm (8.2 in) Diameter: 22 cm (8.6 in)

Ceramic
Nazca (A.D. 1–700)
National Museum of Archaeology, Anthropology and History of Peru, Lima

The upper band of the vessel below right is composed of humanoid faces surrounded by feathers and tentacles. The lower bands of both vessels represent severed human heads.

of thousands, which could be rapidly mobilized thanks to the extensive Inca road network and supply stations, called *tambos*, placed along the routes. Diplomatic negotiations were an important part of Inca war strategy. Annexation of territory often involved bargaining, sometimes with gifts of fine textiles, adornments, and women. Only when such efforts were unsuccessful did Inca armies attack. They became especially ferocious in cases of insurrection. Inca methods of conquest avoided sacking and harm to the population, and neither did they take away their land. Once incorporated, a newly conquered territory had to consent to join the Inca regime and agree to its rules, especially those related to the economic order. The indigenous local leaders were generally retained, but became subservient to the sovereign of Cuzco. Their sons were taken to join the ranks of the provincial nobility in the Inca capital, where they would be treated well and educated in Inca ways.

After winning a conflict, the Incas sang songs of triumph. The cranium of an important enemy killed

(Above, left to right) Woman with Six Fingers on Each Hand
Height: 18 cm (7 in) Diameter: 10 cm (3.9 in)

A Woman of High Rank
Height: 18 cm (7 in) Diameter: 9 cm (3.5 in)

Woman with Six Fingers on Each Hand
Height: 16 cm (6.3 in) Diameter: 10 cm (3.9 in)

Ceramic
Moche (A.D. 50–800)
National Museum of Archaeology, Anthropology and History of Peru, Lima

The bichromatic figures above left and right have six-fingered hands, which may have been related to supernatural forces. The clothing depicted on the center figure indicates a woman of high rank.

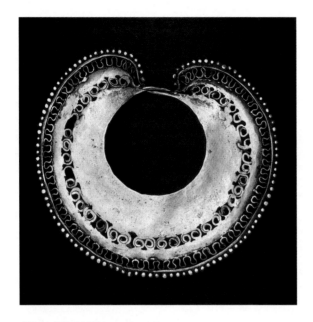

(Above) Gold Filigree Nose Ornament
Vicús (200 B.C.–A.D. 200)
Height: 5 cm (2 in) Width: 6 cm (2.4 in)
National Museum of Archaeology, Anthropology and
History of Peru, Lima

*Nose ornaments were a favorite facial adornment in
ancient Peru. Objects such as the one above were typically
hung from a perforation in the wall of the nose.*

in battle served as a ritual drinking receptacle.
Drums were made with the skin of the conquered,
and necklaces were made from their teeth. Other
spoils of war included trophy heads, which date
back nearly 3,000 years to Chavín. There are many
artistic representations of trophy heads, sometimes
strung together and paraded about, such as those
depicted on Vicús and Recuay ceramics. Drawn with
special frequency on Nazca ceramics are severed
heads that appear in their original size. Trophy
heads like those depicted in Nazca art have been
unearthed from tombs, and these often have a
perforation through which a cord was run, allowing
them to be hung from belts or put in other
prominent locations.

Illnesses and Cures

Illnesses and cures were steeped in the world of
magic for ancient Peruvians. We know this from
information gathered in texts from the sixteenth and

(Opposite, left to right) Pitcher in the Form of a Couple
Height: 19 cm (7.4 in) Diameter: 14 cm (5.5 in)

Pitcher in the Form of a Prisoner
Height: 29 cm (11.3 in) Diameter: 17 cm (6.7 in)

Pitcher in the Form of a Prisoner
Height: 24 cm (9.4 in) Diameter: 15 cm (5.9 in)

Ceramic
Moche (A.D. 50–800)
National Museum of Archaeology, Anthropology and
History of Peru, Lima

(Above, left to right) Double-Body Vase in the Form of a
Seated Man
Height: 14 cm (5.5 in) Diameter: 19 cm (7.6 in)

Whistling Pitcher in the Form of a Man Carrying an
Animal on His Shoulders
Height: 13 cm (5.1 in) Diameter: 11 cm (4.3 in)

Ceramic Sculpture of a Man
Height: 26 cm (10.1 in) Diameter: 9 cm (3.4 in)

Ceramic
Tiahuanaco-Huari (A.D. 200–800)
National Museum of Archaeology, Anthropology and
History of Peru, Lima

*Whistling ceramic vessels were common musical
instruments among the ancient Peruvians.*

(Below) Gold and Silver Ear Ornaments
Sicán (Lambayeque) (A.D. 700–1370)
Height: 7 cm (2.8 in) Diameter: 8 cm (3.2 in)
National Museum of Archaeology, Anthropology and
History of Peru, Lima

(Top left) Pitcher in the Form of a Man Holding a Spondylus Shell
Chancay (A.D. 1200–1450)
Height: 32 cm (12.5 in) Diameter: 20 cm (7.8 in)
National Museum of Archaeology, Anthropology and History of Peru, Lima

Spondylus shells were considered the food of the gods by the ancient Peruvians. They were often used in jewelry and as grave offerings.

(Top right) Pitcher in the Form of a Human Figure Carrying a Severed Head
Height: 24 cm (9.4 in) Diameter: 17 cm (6.7 in)

(Left) Bowl Depicting a Mythical Being
Height: 42 cm (16.4 in) Diameter: 34 cm (13.3 in)

Ceramic
Nazca (A.D. 1–700)
National Museum of Archaeology, Anthropology and History of Peru, Lima

seventeenth centuries, as well as from the practice of folk medicine in contemporary Peru. A comparison of both sources can provide a general understanding of the nature of medicine in ancient Peru.

The basic curative magic of ancient Peru is still practiced today by native masters who are considered to have inherited powers of healing. It should be emphasized, however, that since the time of the conquest, indigenous traditions have been influenced by Spanish folk medicine, and by African traditions. According to ancient and contemporary sources, there were two fundamental causes of illnesses: fright or *jani*, which caused the temporary abandonment of the soul from the body, and harm produced by strangers or occasionally by natural agents or the dead. The healer or shaman was called to help counteract the damage through magic.

Plants were cultivated not only for food consumption and to make clothing and other necessities, but for medicinal purposes as well. The San Pedro cactus was and still is the medicinal hallucinogen of choice along the north coast. It is frequently mixed with other ingredients that strengthen its psychoactive powers.

According to references in early writings, special diets and fasting were common in ancient Peru. Curative substances consisted of concoctions prepared by the healer, who was profoundly versed

(Top left) Carved and Polished Basalt Club Head
Height: 15 cm (5.9 in) Diameter: 12 cm (4.9 in)

(Top right) Carved and Polished Basalt Club Head
Height: 11 cm (4.2 in) Diameter: 8 cm (3.3 in)

Cupisnique (1000–200 B.C.)
National Museum of Archaeology, Anthropology and History of Peru, Lima

(Above left) Carved and Polished Stone Club Head
Inca (A.D. 1200–1532)
Height: 10 cm (3.8 in) Width: 10 cm (3.9 in)
Diameter: 5 cm (1.9 in)
National Museum of Archaeology, Anthropology and History of Peru, Lima

(Above right) Stone Club Head
Chavín (1000–200 B.C.)
Height: 7 cm (2.7 in) Diameter: 16 cm (6.4 in)
National Museum of Archaeology, Anthropology and History of Peru, Lima

(Above) Spear Thrower
Nazca (A.D. 1–700)
Length: 54 cm (21.4 in) Diameter: 1 cm (.4 in)
National Museum of Archaeology, Anthropology and History of Peru, Lima

Spear throwers were used to extend the reach of the arm and create a higher velocity of release for a spear or dart. They were common throughout the Americas.

in herbal traditions. Therapeutics was based on plants and inorganic substances, such as mercury, which were ingested orally. Then, as now, herbalism involved an abundance of plants to which curative properties were attributed.

In addition to the pharmacopoeia, shamans practiced *chupa*, a technique used to extract and cure infections by suctioning the inflicted area with the mouth. Moche ceramics also show cases where a shaman, like a modern doctor, appears to attend to the pains of a reclining patient. The healing of dental cavities through prosthesis was also practiced using copper alloys. These should not be confused, however, with the tradition of beautifying the teeth through the use of metal encrustations, which was also employed.

Trepanation, or cranial drilling, was another ancient medical practice. In Paracas-Cavernas, a culture that developed 2,000 years ago, there were frequent cases of cranial trepanation. The instruments used were obsidian and other stone knives, as well as chisels, probably of bronze. The areas of trepanning were filled with pieces of gourd and, in some cases, with metal plates to protect and help them heal. The wounds were then wrapped with cotton. Different kinds of trepanning included cutting, scraping, sawing, and sectioning. The perforations took different shapes according to the procedure and the instrument employed.

(Above, left to right) Pitcher with Two Linked Scenes
Height: 18 cm (7 in) Diameter: 18 cm (7 in)

Pitcher in the Form of a Reclining Amputee
Height: 18 cm (7 in) Diameter: 16 cm (6.3 in)

Pitcher Depicting the Moche God Aiapaec
Height: 20 cm (7.8 in) Diameter: 18 cm (7 in)

Pitcher Depicting a Healer
Height: 20 cm (7.8 in) Diameter: 17 cm (6.6 in)

Ceramic
Moche (A.D. 50–800)
National Museum of Archaeology, Anthropology and History of Peru, Lima

In the upper part of the pitcher at far left, two blind men are shown. In the lower section, figures of death dance in the underworld. In addition to having his feet amputated, the lips of the victim depicted second from left were also mutilated, probably to draw blood that was offered to a divinity as a sacrifice. On the pitcher third from left, Aiapaec, wearing a headdress, stands in a trance, accompanied by two attendants.

(Top, left to right) Pitcher Depicting a Bird-Man Warrior
Height: 31 cm (12.1 in) Diameter: 16 cm (6.2 in)

Pitcher Depicting Hand-to-Hand Combat
Height: 28 cm (10.9 in) Diameter: 16 cm (6.2 in)

Pitcher Depicting a Supernatural Being in the Form of
the Moon
Height: 29 cm (11.3 in) Diameter: 15 cm (5.9 in)

(Above left) Pitcher Depicting Weapons of Combat
Height: 30 cm (11.7 in) Diameter: 16 cm (6.2 in)

(Above right) Pitcher with Symbolic Designs
Height: 29 cm (11.3 in) Diameter: 16 cm (6.3 in)

(Above) Pitcher in the Form of a Bloated Amputated
Human Leg
Height: 14 cm (5.5 in) Diameter: 20 cm (7.8 in)

Ceramic
Moche (A.D. 50–800)
National Museum of Archaeology, Anthropology and
History of Peru, Lima

*The amputated limb depicted in this monochromatic
stirrup-spout vessel appears fat or swollen. The precise use
of these vessels is unknown, but they may have been used
as votive offerings in prayer for the healing of a stricken
body part.*

(Above, left) Cosmetically Deformed Cranium

(Above, right) Cosmetically Deformed Cranium with Trepanation

Paracas (700 B.C.–A.D. 1)
National Museum of Archaeology, Anthropology and History of Peru, Lima

Before the advent of modern medicine, the people of ancient Peru practiced a primitive form of cranial surgery through trepanation, the cutting of portions of the skull. Unlike other ancient civilizations in Africa and Europe, for example, where trepanation was performed on the skulls of those already deceased for superstitious reasons, the trepaned skulls of ancient Peru reveal that the procedure was carried out on the living to treat head injuries and relieve such ailments as epilepsy and headaches. Cranial operations began in ancient Peru as early as 400 B.C., and, as surgeons' techniques became more refined, the success rate increased, with more than half of those who received excisions surviving the procedure.

(Opposite, left) Deformed Cranium with Trepanation
Paracas (700 B.C.–A.D. 1)
National Museum of Archaeology, Anthropology and History of Peru, Lima

(Opposite, top) Cranium with a Large Bone Tumor
Paucarcancha origin, Cuzco
National Museum of Archaeology, Anthropology and History of Peru, Lima

(Opposite, bottom right) Cranium with Five Trepanations
Unknown origin
National Museum of Archaeology, Anthropology and History of Peru, Lima

To access the brain, Peruvian surgeons employed tools such as knives, tweezers, chisels, hammers, and scalpels to scrape, cut, and drill into the cranium. The skull opposite left reveals an enormous trepaned opening extending across the frontal and parietal bones. Despite the enormous hole, there is obvious regrowth around the edges, indicating that the patient lived for some time following the surgery. Contrasted with more primitive rectangular cutting, the circular excisions shown bottom right indicate the most evolved and successful form of trepanation.

Crossed incisions allowed for the removal of square bone fragments. Other configurations were polygonal, circular, or oval. On some occasions, an individual underwent multiple trepanning. Evidence gathered from scarring reveals that a remarkable number of people survived the operations, which is startling especially given the extent of the perforation.

Trepanation was one of the few health practices that is easily discerned in the archaeological record. Undoubtedly the prehistoric people of the Andes had a large repertoire of practices and products they used to ensure their health, which typifies the sophisticated approach the early Andean people had to their worlds, both natural and cultural.

(Below) Obsidian Tools Used for Cranial Trepanation
Paracas (700 B.C.–A.D. 1)
National Museum of Archaeology, Anthropology and History of Peru, Lima

Trepanation, the surgical removal of portions of living skull, was practiced by Peruvians more than 2,000 years ago. The ancient blades shown below were used to excise circular, square, or irregular shaped pieces of the skull.

Textiles

The art of textile making in Peru has a brilliant history dating back thousands of years. Textiles were a highly treasured commodity, in part because of the large amount of labor and care that went into making them. Fine fabrics were prized to such an extent that they became regulated by the state under the Incas, and were the preferred royal gift. The quality of the fabric in the clothing Andean people wore, as well as the motifs and iconography displayed on it, signified both social status and cultural identity. In the cordilleras, where the temperature was cold after the sun set, wool from various camelids was preferred. Alpaca was considered finer than llama wool, and vicuña was considered superior to both. In the hot regions of the coastal area cotton was the preferred material. Human hair, feathers, and metal plates were sometimes used to decorate surfaces of fabric. Netting, a technique for making textiles without a loom, employed loops and knots in the creation of the fabric, and its origins may have been in the invention of the fishing net, an essential tool for early Peruvians who settled along the coast, where textile manufacture is thought to have begun.

From the coastal cultures of Paracas and Chancay come particularly beautiful textiles. Many survived for hundreds of years in the arid coastal climate buried as wrappings around mummies. Mummy wrappings such as those found at Paracas Necropolis had special significance. The bodies of older males were wrapped in the most exquisite fabrics, indicating high status. Patterns and images of plants and animals may have conveyed information about the deceased's lineage, role in society, and occupation.

The Early Horizon was a time of great inventiveness in textile design and manufacture as seen in the Chavín culture. The heddle loom came into use around this time, a device that raised and lowered warps so that wefts could be easily inserted. Chavín textile design and iconography probably established the wearer's allegiance to the Chavín cult. Textiles were discovered in the seaside cemetery of Karwa, for example, that were probably religious banners. They display the Chavín style, and incorporate many of the images from Chavín iconography.

(Above) Pitcher with a Sculpted Head Depicting a Man Chewing Coca Leaves
Moche (A.D. 50–800)
Height: 26 cm (10.2 in) Diameter: 18 cm (7 in)
National Museum of Archaeology, Anthropology and History of Peru, Lima

Coca leaves were chewed by the ancient Peruvians to help them develop stamina and improve their adaptation to altitude, and as a mild social drug. The man depicted in the vessel above carries a bag for coca leaves on his back. He is shown using a small spatula to add a pinch of ash or lime to the coca as a catalyzing agent.

(Opposite) Woven Poncho (Unku) with Symbolic Motifs
Tiahuanaco-Huari (A.D. 200–800)
Width: 104 cm (41 in) Length: 104 cm (41 in)
National Museum of Archaeology, Anthropology and History of Peru, Lima

(Above) Poncho with Fringe and Decorative Borders
Nazca (A.D. 1–700)
Width: 57 cm (22.6 in) Length: 77 cm (30.4 in)
National Museum of Archaeology, Anthropology and
History of Peru, Lima

(Left) Woven Four-Pointed Cap with Symbolic Motifs
Tiahuanaco-Huari (A.D. 200–800)
Width: 15 cm (5.9 in) Length: 15 cm (5.9 in)
National Museum of Archaeology, Anthropology and
History of Peru, Lima

*This typical four-pointed Huari cap is often represented on
painted ceramics.*

(Bottom left) Border Band with Symbolic Three-
Dimensional Figures
Nazca (A.D. 1–700)
Width: 5 cm (2 in) Length: 50 cm (19.5 in)
National Museum of Archaeology, Anthropology and
History of Peru, Lima

Textiles

Colorful paints were applied directly to these textiles. On these banners, however, the Chavín Staff God was depicted as a woman. Archaeologist Richard Burger has speculated that the Karwa Staff Goddess may have been the sister, daughter, or wife of the great Staff God of Chavín de Huántar.

Use of the backstrap loom dates back at least to the Moche. This device was made of two rods with the warp threads stretched between them. One end of each loom was tied to a tall wooden support, the other to a belt around the weaver's waist. By leaning back, the weaver could control the tension of the threads. Fabric made from backstrap looms spanned no more than an arm's length, as far as the weaver could reach in passing the weft thread through the warp.

In Inca society, the most common fabric used for clothing was called *huasca*, and was made of cotton or alpaca wool. Decorative patterns were woven into this fabric, sometimes combining the natural hues of the cotton with colorful tints from natural substances. Reds came from animal resources, and yellows came from the bark of the

(Above) Mantle with Images of a Supernatural Being
Paracas (700 B.C.–A.D. 1)
Width: 143 cm (56.2 in) Length: 289 cm (113.9 in)
National Museum of Archaeology, Anthropology and History of Peru, Lima

This woven polychrome cape, with flat-point border, features the most important Paracas deity in the form of an anthropomorphic winged figure. Surrounding the deity are serpents and severed heads.

(Left) Woven Cloth Fragment with Stylized Feline Heads and Decorative Motifs
Tiahuanaco-Huari (A.D. 200–800)
Width: 36 cm (14 in) Length: 49 cm (19.1 in)
National Museum of Archaeology, Anthropology and History of Peru, Lima

(Above) Woven Mantle with Images of Felines
Paracas (Necropolis) (700 B.C.–A.D. 1)
Width: 42 cm (16.4 in) Length: 50 cm (19.5 in)
National Museum of Archaeology, Anthropology and
History of Peru, Lima

This polychrome cloak, with fringe on two sides, has
embroidered motifs depicting felines on square fields.

(Right) Jar with Lid
Recuay (A.D. 1–650)
Height: 28 cm (11.1 in) Diameter: 23 cm (9.1 in)
National Museum of Archaeology, Anthropology and
History of Peru, Lima

Typical of the Recuay style, this vessel was made without
handles, and was probably intended to be held in both hands.
Repeated designs are shown on four horizontal bands. The
lowest band displays a two-headed serpent, a prevalent
Andean motif thought to be symbolic of the rainbow.

Textiles

(Above left) Belts Woven from Wool and Cotton
Chancay (A.D. 1200–1450)
Width: 10 cm (3.9 in) Length: 471 cm (185.6 in)
Amano Museum Foundation, Lima

(Above) Woven Bag with Two-Headed Bird Motif
South Coast (n.d.)
Width: 14 cm (5.5 in) Length: 16 cm (6.2 in)
National Museum of Archaeology, Anthropology and
History of Peru, Lima

(Left) Miniature Poncho with Stylized Bird Motif (detail)
South Coast (n.d.)
Width: 24 cm (9.4 in) Length: 23 cm (9 in)
National Museum of Archaeology, Anthropology and
History of Peru, Lima

(Above, left) Woven Cloth with Positive and Negative Stylized Feline Figures
Chancay (A.D. 1200–1450)
Width: 40 cm (15.6 in) Length: 74 cm (29.3 in)
National Museum of Archaeology, Anthropology and History of Peru, Lima

(Above) Woven Bag with Tassels and Geometric Motifs
Inca (A.D. 1200–1532)
Width: 16 cm (6.2 in) Length: 21 cm (8.2 in)
National Museum of Archaeology, Anthropology and History of Peru, Lima

Tassels and symbolic designs embellish this polychrome chuspa.

(Left) Woven Tapestry Depicting Supernatural Beings (detail)
Chancay (A.D. 1200–1450)
Width: 10 cm (3.9 in) Length: 46 cm (18.3 in)
Amano Museum Foundation, Lima

Textiles

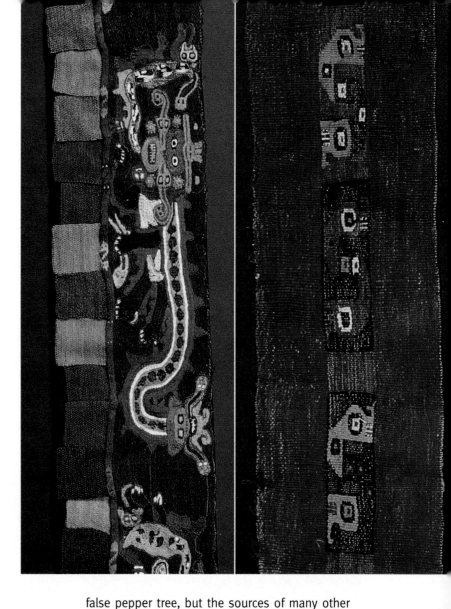

(Right) Belt Woven from Wool and Cotton
Chancay (A.D. 1200–1450)
Width: 10 cm (3.9 in) Length: 470 cm (184.9 in)
Amano Museum Foundation, Lima

(Far right) Woven Textile with Double-Headed Serpent-Feline Motif
Tiahuanaco-Huari (A.D. 200–800)
Width: 52 cm (20.3 in) Length: 61 cm (24.2 in)
National Museum of Archaeology, Anthropology and History of Peru, Lima

On this polychrome belt fragment there appears a two-headed serpent-feline, perhaps a precedent for the popular two-headed symbol.

(Below) Woven Poncho with a Decorative Border
Chancay (A.D. 1200–1450)
Width: 59 cm (23.4 in) Length: 51 cm (19.9 in)
National Museum of Archaeology, Anthropology and History of Peru, Lima

The decorative border on this unku, *or poncho-like garment, depicts three bands of symbolic motifs, including a line of sea birds surrounded by stylized ocean waves.*

false pepper tree, but the sources of many other dyes remain unknown. The finest fabric made by the Inca was known as *cumbi*, and was reserved exclusively for the emperor and the privileged individuals who received it from him. Made of soft fibers dyed in a wide range of colors, and then woven into standard geometric patterns, cumbi garments established the wearer's rank. Women of all social classes in ancient Peru were weavers, though cord and rope were typically made by men. Professional weavers and wives of provincial officials produced cumbi as a tax payment. Special cumbi garments made for sacred rites and worn by the emperor were usually made by *aclla*, women in religious service.

Hand-woven textiles continue to be important in contemporary Peru, and are often used in rituals designed to placate the spirits of ancestors and the forces of nature.

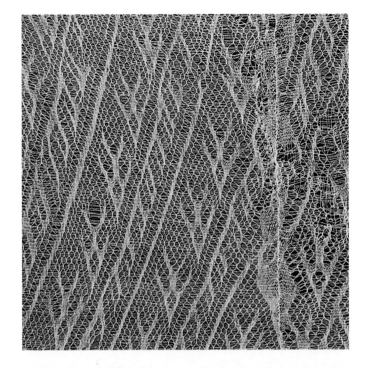

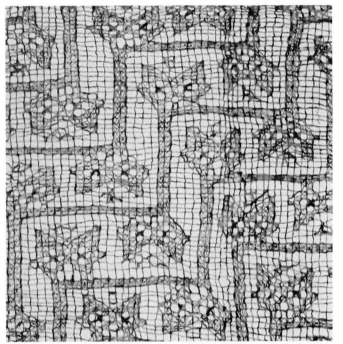

(Top row, left to right) Netted Cotton Textile with Geometric Designs
Chancay (A.D. 1200–1450)
Width: 85 cm (33.5 in) Length: 75 cm (29.6 in)
Amano Museum Foundation, Lima

Woven Textile Fragment with Images of Llamas and People
Inca (A.D. 1200–1532)
Width: 147 cm (57.7 in) Length: 130 cm (51.1 in)
National Museum of Archaeology, Anthropology and History of Peru, Lima

Netted Cotton Textile with Geometric Designs
Chancay (A.D. 1200–1450)
Width: 79 cm (31.2 in) Length: 89 cm (35.1 in)
Amano Museum Foundation, Lima

(Center row, left to right) Woven Cotton Textile with Stylized Feline Designs
Chancay (A.D. 1200–1450)
Width: 33 cm (12.9 in) Length: 100 cm (39.4 in)
Amano Museum Foundation, Lima

Painted Fabric with Stylized Bird Motifs
Chancay (A.D. 1200–1450)
Width: 135 cm (53 in) Length: 382 cm (150.4 in)
National Museum of Archaeology, Anthropology and History of Peru, Lima

Netted Cotton Cloth with Stylized Feline Faces
Chancay (A.D. 1200–1450)
Width: 62 cm (24.6 in) Length: 91 cm (35.9 in)
National Museum of Archaeology, Anthropology and History of Peru, Lima

(Bottom row, left to right) Netted Cotton Textile with Stylized Felines and Ocean Waves
Chancay (A.D. 1200–1450)
Width: 46 cm (18.3 in) Length: 95 cm (37.3 in)
Amano Museum Foundation, Lima

Netted Cotton Textile with Representations of Supernatural Beings, Felines and Ocean Waves
Chancay (A.D. 1200–1450)
Width: 86 cm (33.9 in) Length: 196 cm (37.8 in)
Amano Museum Foundation, Lima

Netted Cotton Textile with Stylized Representations of Felines and Ocean Waves
Chancay (A.D. 1200–1450)
Width: 78 cm (30.8 in) Length: 89 cm (35.1 in)
Amano Museum Foundation, Lima

Death and Burial

The subject of death in ancient Peru encompasses a wide spectrum of beliefs and practices, including diverse ceremonies, funerary rites, methods of burial, and mummification techniques, all of which have their origins in the mist of prehistory. As reflected in archaeological, ethnohistorical, and ethnographic records, the cult of the dead played a significant role in ancient Peruvian society. Archaeological evidence reveals that the dead were buried in many ways, for example in various types of pyramids and tombs, and in pits, caves, and wrapped in multiple layers of cloth. Documents about the Incas from the sixteenth and seventeenth centuries by Spanish authors like Pedro Cieza de León, and mestizos like Garcilaso de la Vega and Felipe Guamán Poma de Ayala, help us to complete the picture of the afterlife offered in the archaeological record. Although the evidence they offer must be approached critically, their writing tells us much about rituals such as the *pacaricuy*, or wake, and the pompous ceremony associated with it; norms observed during funerals; the *puruc raya*, an annual ceremony held in memory of deceased ancestors; and other practices related to Andean funerary rites.

Then, as now, the dead were mourned during the period of the wake, and as the mummified remains were carried to the place of burial. On these occasions, mourning was accompanied by recitation of the virtues and achievements of the deceased. The

(Above) Unwrapped Mummy in the Fetal Position
Origin unknown
National Museum of Archaeology, Anthropology and
History of Peru, Lima

Around this mummy is the rope ancient Peruvians used to bind the deceased into fetal positions. The hair has been treated with spices.

(Opposite) Mask for a Mummy Bundle
Wood
Chancay (A.D. 1200–1450)
Height: 29 cm (11.3 in) Width: 22 cm (8.7 in)
National Museum of Archaeology, Anthropology and
History of Peru, Lima

In preparation for burial, mummified bodies were first wrapped in fine textiles, then covered in a large plain cloth. Painted masks like the one opposite were then placed on the wrapped bundle.

body was mummified in a squatting or fetal position, then wrapped in cloth until the bundle resembled a seated person. It was then placed in an individual or collective tomb, accompanied by funerary goods such as ceramic pitchers containing liquid offerings. Illustrious male deceased would also be accompanied by their wives or concubines, who might have been ritually killed or sacrificed.

Ancient beliefs about *piccha*, or the presence of the spirit of the deceased for five days after death, have survived to this day, as has the custom of offering food at graves on the anniversary of a person's death as a way of symbolically sharing with them the food they preferred in life.

The dead, mummified and revered, were expected to implore the supernatural powers for the needs of the living: soil fertility, water, and the multiplication of domestic animals. Bodies were sometimes buried in cultivated fields in order to enrich them. According to sixteenth-century chroniclers, such so-called strengthening rites were also practiced in laying the foundations of buildings.

(Opposite) Mask for a Mummy Bundle
Wood
Chancay (A.D. 1200–1450)
Height: 25 cm (9.9 in) Width: 19 cm (7.4 in)
National Museum of Archaeology, Anthropology and History of Peru, Lima

(Top right) Tomb Guardian Mask
Ceramic and straw
Chachapoyas (A.D. 1000–1470)
Height: 66 cm (26 in) Width: 15 cm (5.9 in)
National Museum of Archaeology, Anthropology and History of Peru, Lima

This mask sat atop one of the large humanoid figures that guarded a grotto high on the walls of a ravine in the Andes. The mask wears a conical hat on which a ritual cranium could have been mounted.

(Bottom right) Dance or Ritual Mask
Ceramic
Moche (A.D. 50–800)
Height: 19 cm (7.6 in) Width: 17 cm (6.5 in)
National Museum of Archaeology, Anthropology and History of Peru, Lima

(Above) Unwrapped Mummy in the Fetal Position
Origin unknown
National Museum of Archaeology, Anthropology and
History of Peru, Lima

Burial in the fetal position may indicate that the dead await
rebirth. (Below) A mummy bundle from Huallamarca such
as the one that contained the mummified woman with
long hair (opposite).

With few exceptions (among the Moche, for example) bodies were buried as though seated, and the hands frequently held the head, perhaps to simulate the fetal position. After placement of the mummy in the tomb or burial site, various rituals were observed to ensure that the soul would not return home.

In Inca society, an important group of descendants, the *panaca,* had the responsibility of caring for the mummies of deceased royalty, which were attended for generations. Pizzaro's secretary, Pedro Sancho, wrote that "each dead [Inca] lord has here [in Cuzco] his house with everything in it that he had in life, since no ruler who succeeds him may take possession of his inheritance." Later, Garcilaso described with amazement the expressions on the faces of the mummies of Inca lords he visited before leaving Cuzco. The mummified bodies of Inca monarchs were periodically brought out as part of a procession through the main plaza of the city.

Theories abound regarding ancient Peruvian embalming techniques. It can be assumed, however, that most mummies were dried naturally. While some bodies may have been cured over a fire or treated with plant materials, the cold and dry climate of the mountains and the dry heat of the coast were important factors in their preservation. These same drying processes also mummified organs and viscera, eyes, the brain mass, as well as the soft and fatty tissues of the body. Some mummies conserve even the prepuce, eyelashes, nails, and hair.

Life Beyond the Grave

The lengths to which ancient Peruvians went to preserve the bodies of their dead constitutes irrefutable proof of a firm conviction that when an individual died, a new phase of existence awaited him or her. Our knowledge regarding the Peruvian concept of life beyond the grave, however, is unfortunately rather limited. Some glimpses are presented in images painted some 1,500 years ago on Moche ceramics. In these representations, the deceased, though depicted as skeletons, appear to be dancing, holding hands, or playing flutes and other musical instruments. In some cases, the facial expressions of these "living dead" seem to indicate that they might be intoxicated or entranced. Moche iconography also includes amorous scenes that take place in macabre settings beyond the grave, some of which may be related to fertility rites.

Although belief in an afterlife was pervasive in ancient Peru, it seems that neither a heaven nor a hell was thought to await the deceased. Father Pablo Joseph de Arriaga concluded in 1621 that "they did not distinguish that [in the afterlife] there must be punishment for the bad or bliss for the good." The absence of a belief in reward or condemnation in the afterlife confirms the fact that the religious structure in ancient Peru was separate from moral concerns.

Certain ethnohistorical sources note a belief that the dead lived on in the *upamarca*, a land of silence reached only after the deceased had spent five days as a ghost in the place where he or she had lived. Father Arriaga also points to a native idea of the afterlife as a "house of rest." Such a belief, however, would seem at odds with the images found in Moche iconography. Other sources suggest that the afterlife was not a place of rest. In his *Sermons*, for example, Francisco de Avila indicates that there was a belief that the deceased went to "a ravine or valley, and that they live there, working, drinking, and eating, and the women grind in the mills." The milling stones, principal items used in food preparation, were commonly included as burial offerings.

In general, existence in the afterlife seems to have been imagined as a continuation of the kind of life the individual had experienced while living. Commoners continued to work the land, and nobles continued to rule over their subjects and retain their privileges. Father Arriaga is emphatic in this regard: "They do not know in this life nor in the other more happiness than to have good *chácara* [sown land], from which they can eat and

Mummy of a Woman with Long Hair
National Museum of Archaeology, Anthropology and History of Peru, Huallamarca Museum

This mummy was exhumed from the uppermost platform of Lima's Huaca Huallamarca, a shrine that later became a burial site. Several burial methods have been discovered at the site, reflecting different eras of occupation. The method of burial for this mummy corresponds to Middle Horizon culture. The bodies of their dead were usually interred in a flexed position, wrapped in a series of cotton textiles. A face on the bundle, typically painted red with black eyes, had a wooden nose and hair made from plant fiber. Scientific analysis reveals that this was a person thirty to thirty-five years of age. She measures 4 feet 9 inches in height, and has hair 6 feet 6 inches in length. Her left arm is tattooed with a bird design. It has been determined that she did not have an active life, but spent most of her time in a squatting position. She was possibly a weaver. She was not buried with rich goods, but wears a cotton tunic of natural color that was highly valued. Near her body were the remains of a macaw, a bird highly prized for its bright plumage, which was sometimes presented as an offering.

Clide Valladolid
Director, Proyecto Arqueológico, Huallamarca

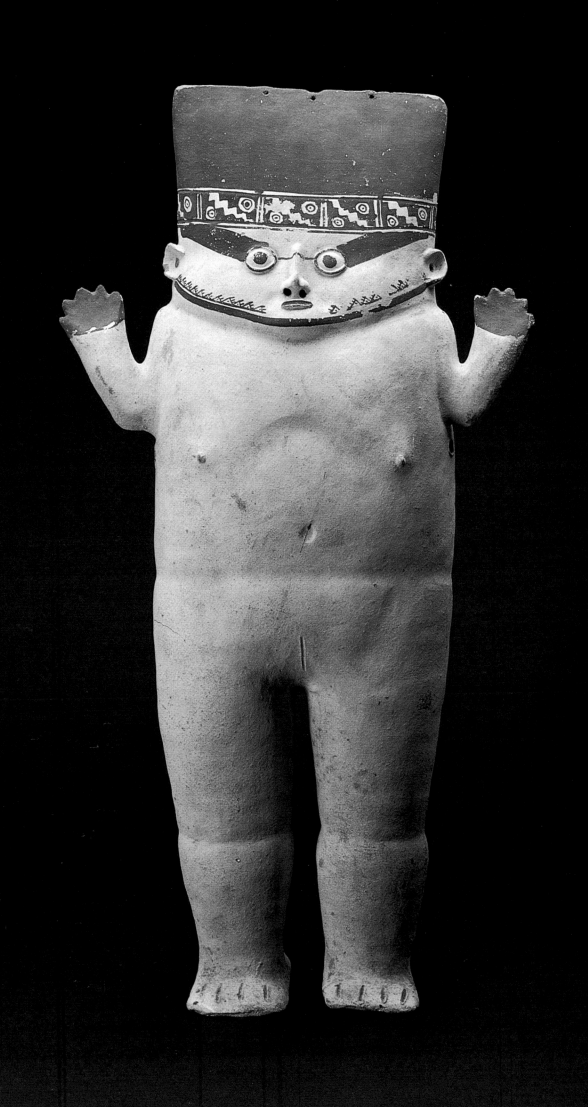

drink, and so it is said that [the dead] go to sow land." Concerning the privileges enjoyed in life, he added that "when the Incas died, killed and interred with them were women, so that in the other life they could prepare *chicha,* along with weavers and sandal menders, that they might serve them there."

Beliefs varied concerning where the dead traveled in the afterlife. It is thought, for example, that the people of the sierra believed that after the *piccha* period of five days had expired, the deceased crossed a river, with the help of black

(Opposite and above) Female Supernatural Beings
Ceramic
Chancay (A.D. 1200–1450)
Height: 60 cm (23.8 in) Diameter: 33 cm (12.9 in)
National Museum of Archaeology, Anthropology and History of Peru, Lima

These bichromatic effigy jars depict a female supernatural deity popularly known as chuchimilco.

dogs, by a narrow bridge made of hair. The coastal people believed that the deceased were taken to the guano islands by sea lions. The people of the southern ranges supposed that the dead ended up on the mountain of Coropuna. Fragments of ancient beliefs transmitted by Pedro Cieza de León in 1553 tell us that the people who lived near the ancient sanctuary of Ausangate in Cuzco were certain that "the souls that left their bodies went to a great lake, where their vain beliefs gave way to the understanding that this was their origin, and from there they entered into the bodies of those who were being born."

The extreme care taken in the preservation of the cadaver by ancient Peruvians may point to a belief that the existence of the *carcanchas* or "animated dead" continued indefinitely, so long as the cadaver was not annihilated by putrefaction, fire, or other agents. If a calamity were to befall the body of the deceased, it may have been thought that existence in the afterlife would cease forever.

The Supernatural World

The people of the Andes show a predilection toward mysticism and ceremony. Even today, Andeans are steeped in an elaborate religious tradition. A significant part of this may be explained by ecological factors. As we have already noted, perhaps no other agricultural society in the world has had to face a more difficult environment. The effort made by ancient Peruvians to overcome the harsh environment through hard labor and technical prowess was not enough. Combating an endemic state of crisis was also thought to require intense religious practice.

The dramatic situation created by the environment perhaps explains why Andean religious beliefs were unencumbered by the moralizing typical of other religious traditions. The deities of the ancient Peruvians were considered fundamental gods of sustenance rather than moral enforcers. Laws against stealing and adultery were, of course, enforced, but these were crimes against the state, and it was the duty of the administrators of state law to punish offenders. There was no concept of a future expiation. The relationship between religion and morality was closest with regard to behavior toward the deities: If worship of the gods was not properly carried out, they were affronted, resulting in a series of disasters that could only be checked through supplication and sacrifice.

Not many details of pre-Inca religion are known. What is known comes primarily from what the Spanish observed of the Incas. The gods of Inca religion, and probably most pre-Inca religions, personified or controlled the forces of nature, and though individualized and hierarchical, they functioned collectively with regard to the economic condition of the people. The most popular and universal god was the male deity Illapa. Associated with meteorological phenomena, such as thunder, lightning, clouds, and rainbows, Illapa personified rain. As the direct source of sustenance, bringing rain to the highlands, rivers, and rich alluvial soils in the

(Above) Whistling Pitcher Depicting a
Kneeling Woman
Moche (A.D. 50–800)
Height: 19 cm (7.4 in) Diameter: 19 cm (7.4 in)
National Museum of Archaeology,
Anthropology and History of Peru, Lima

Whistling ceramic vessels were common musical instruments among the ancient Peruvians. The eyes and ears have been left open to emit sounds made by blowing across the spout of the pitcher.

(Opposite) Pitcher Representing the Moche God Aiapaec (detail)
Moche (A.D. 50–800)
Height: 31 cm (12.1 in) Diameter: 26 cm (10.2 in)
National Museum of Archaeology, Anthropology and History
of Peru, Lima

coastal valleys, Illapa was revered, yet also feared for the crash of his thunder, for his sometimes deadly lightning, for catastrophic hailstorms, and severe floods. The worst of his scourges was drought. Proof of Illapa's status was the major temple dedicated to him in Cuzco. According to the plan of Cuzco drawn by Guamán Poma, and the description of it written by the seventeenth-century chronicler Cristobal de Molina, Illapa's temple was rivaled only by the Coricancha, the Temple of the Sun.

Illapa was often depicted as a feline, and may, according to iconographical studies, represent a sort of universal god of the Andes that dates back to Chavín culture. The image on El Lanzón at Chavín de Huántar can be considered an archetypal form of the feline, and may represent Illapa. The presence of feline features imparts demonic traits to Illapa. These are especially evident in the mouth and in the lips, which are often pulled back in a snarl to reveal fangs. This demonic expression carried over into other cultures, especially in representations of the Moche god Aiapaec.

(Above, left) Double-Bodied Whistling Pitcher
Ceramic
Vicús (200 B.C.–A.D. 200)
Height: 21 cm (8.2 in) Diameter: 20 cm (7.8 in)
National Museum of Archaeology, Anthropology and History of Peru, Lima

Atop the front chamber of this whistling pitcher rests a dwelling enclosed by three walls that have a stepped design. The roof of the structure slopes toward the rear of the dwelling. Four pyramidal shapes adorn the roof.

(Left) Pitcher Depicting a Scene of Human Sacrifice to the Moche God Aiapaec
Ceramic
Moche (A.D. 50–800)
Height: 23 cm (9 in) Diameter: 17 cm (6.6 in)
National Museum of Archaeology, Anthropology and History of Peru, Lima

Aiapaec, distinguished by his feline mouth and semi-circular headdress, watches as individuals sacrificially hurl themselves from the mountain peaks.

In contemporary Peruvian folklore, Illapa's cult still flourishes in the veneration of the hills and high mountains where the falcon nests, places sacred to this deity. Qoa, one of a variety of modern names, still appears as a flying cat, or tiger bird, his eyes throwing out lightning and his urine transformed into rain. Also associated with Illapa are the *apus*, the spirits of the mountains and lakes, which, if they are not worshiped, make the waves rise destructively, and which are offended if approached by someone not protected by the sacred coca leaf.

Viracocha was considered the universal creator who caused the sun to emerge from Lake Titicaca. Then he went on to Tiahuanaco, where he molded animals and men from clay. In a prayer to him recorded by Cristobal de Molina, Viracocha is surrounded by "thunder and tempests." It was also believed that he could cause water to flow from rocks.

Pachacamac, animator of the world, is also linked with creation. He is characterized primarily as the bearer of the food necessary for survival as a result of the entreaties of a primordial woman,

(Above, right) Pitcher Depicting the Moche God Aiapaec
Ceramic
Moche (A.D. 50–800)
Height: 31 cm (12.1 in) Diameter: 11 cm (10.2 in)
National Museum of Archaeology, Anthropology and History of Peru, Lima

With the mouth of a feline, Aiapaec is depicted standing in front of an apu, *or sacred mountain. Aiapaec, the powerful one, is supported by two serpents, which may represent rivers and valleys.*

(Right) Pitcher Depicting a Supernatural Being
Ceramic
Nazca (A.D. 1–700)
Height: 61 cm (24.2 in) Diameter: 46 cm (18.3 in)
National Museum of Archaeology, Anthropology and History of Peru, Lima

An anthropomorphic supernatural figure with symbolic attributes is depicted on this semi-sculpted vessel. The mustache, composed of two stylized birds, is suggestive of feline whiskers. Decorating the body are painted symbols of snakes with feline heads, as well as severed human heads.

(Above, left to right) Pitcher with an Image of a Deity
Height: 23 cm (9 in) Diameter: 18 cm (7 in)

Pitcher in the Form of a Supernatural Feline with Human
Features
Height: 17 cm (6.6 in) Diameter: 10 cm (3.8 in)

Pitcher with Representations of Supernatural Beings
Holding a Severed Human Head
Height: 18 cm (7 in) Diameter: 14 cm (5.5 in)

Ceramic
Nazca (A.D. 1–700)
National Museum of Archaeology, Anthropology and
History of Peru, Lima

*The Nazca penchant for mythical themes, inherited from
Paracas culture, is evident in the three pieces shown above.
The upper portion of the double-spouted vessel above left
features a colorful representation of a widespread Andean
divinity with bird and human features. The vessel above
right depicts a figure made up of feline, bird, and human
features. The arms and hands of the creature are extended
and hold a severed head by the hair, which the figure may
be about to eat, as evidenced by its protruding tongue. The
face on the sculpted effigy vessel in the center has a feline
mustache that frames the nostrils and eyebrows. From his
hands hang acidic fruits. These images were burnished onto
the surface of the vessels in the late stages of drying, which
explains the smooth shiny surface on these and on most
Nazca vessels.*

Pachamama, Mother Earth. The provision of edible
plants is related in other myths. In one of these,
Pachacamac disguises himself as the sun, and with
his rays fertilizes the primordial woman, perhaps
the incarnation of Pachamama. In another myth,
Pachacamac kills what he has created, and this
action may be interpreted as the institution of
human sacrifice as a means of providing
nourishment to the food and fertility deities. When
the victim is buried, his teeth sprout maize, his
bones become manioc, and so on.

Images discovered by archaeologists indicate that
the ultimate masculine creative force was
incarnated in Inti, the Sun God. He offered heat
and light, and his rays possessed fertilizing powers.
Mythic literature testifies to the reliance of the
Andean people on the power of the sun, and to
their anxiety that it could disappear, causing a
cataclysm and the destruction of humankind,
followed by the creation of a new generation of
human beings. This anxiety explains the redoubled
prayers and supplications that reportedly took
place during solar eclipses, rituals that ended with
loud cries and lamentations. Even domestic
animals were said to have been whipped to make
them howl.

Gold was the symbol of the sun, and the robes
of leading priests were covered with fluttering
metal disks that reflected the sun's rays and

imitated its radiance. Inti is also associated with Illapa, as both the sun and rain are necessary for a fertile earth. In visual representations, particularly those at Chavín and Tiahuanaco, Inti appears with big teardrops that undoubtedly symbolize rain.

Pachamama, Mother Earth, symbolized the feminine element of divinity for the Andean people. As the primordial mother, she is sometimes personified as Quilla, the moon, and symbolized by silver. Many images of Pachamama, especially in the form of a half-moon, appear in silver. The cult of Pachamama was, and still is, extensive. Ancient documents show that Pachamama was frequently individualized to guarantee the abundance of specific crops. In Andean iconography there are representations of Pachamama incarnated in specific vegetable forms: multiple ears of maize, for instance, or groups of potatoes.

The mythological literature tells of several other female supernatural beings, who were likely regional versions of Pachamama. Among them are Chaupiñanca, the primordial mother of Huarochiri mythology; Illa, who appears in the mythic traditions of the Ecuadorian Andes; and Urpihuachac, sister and wife of Pachacamac, who seems to be an expression of Cochamama, the marine form of Pachamama who is said to have created fish and seabirds. Pachamama in her Cochamama form also appears to symbolize abundant water.

Pachamama still plays an important role in the deeply rooted peasant magic of today's Andean

(Above) Pitcher Depicting the Moche God Aiapaec
Ceramic
Moche (A.D. 50–800)
Height: 24 cm (9.4)
National Museum of Archaeology, Anthropology and History of Peru, Lima

The arched handle on this vessel is painted with geometric motifs. A wave emblem radiates from the head of the Moche god Aiapaec, who wears a necklace or collar with circular shapes that may also represent water.

(Below, left to right) Pitcher Depicting a Flying Fox-Man Warrior
Height: 24 cm (9.4 in) Diameter: 15 cm (5.9 in)

Pitcher with Mythical Scene in Relief
Height: 24 cm (9.4 in) Diameter: 16 cm (6.2 in)

Pitcher Depicting a Bird-Man Warrior in a Ritual Race or Dance
Height: 30 cm (11.7 in) Diameter: 17 cm (6.7 in)

Ceramic
Moche (A.D. 50–800)
National Museum of Archaeology, Anthropology and History of Peru, Lima

These three vessels depict action scenes in which the distinction between humans and animals is blurred. The central object depicts, in low relief, the Moche god Aiapaec combating a giant crab with human attributes. On the right is a stirrup-spout bottle depicting a ritual race in which the participants exhibit human, lobster, and bird features. The arched stirrup-spout bottle at far left shows a running warrior with human and fox or dog attributes.

(Above, left to right) Pitcher in the Form of the God Aiapaec
Ceramic
Moche (A.D. 50–800)
Height: 24 cm (9.3 in) Diameter: 17 cm (6.8 in)
National Museum of Archaeology, Anthropology and
History of Peru, Lima

This vessel depicts the Moche god Aiapaec seated, holding a shield in his hand, with a menacing expression, a typical feature distinguishing Moche gods. He is adorned with symbolic earrings, a pectoral, and an ostentatious headdress in the shape of a bird.

Pitcher in the Form of a Swimmer
Moche (A.D. 50–800)
Height: 16 cm (6.3 in) Width: 9 cm (3.1 in)
National Museum of Archaeology, Anthropology and
History of Peru, Lima

(Opposite, top left) Silver Ocarina with the Figure of
a Deer
Chimú (A.D. 1100–1450)
Height: 15 cm (5.9 in) Width: 12 cm (4.75 in)
National Museum of Archaeology, Anthropology and
History of Peru, Lima

(Opposite, top right) Pitcher with a Relief Sculpture of the
Moche God Aiapaec
Ceramic
Moche (A.D. 50–800)
Height: 25 cm (9.8 in) Diameter: 14 cm (5.5 in)
National Museum of Archaeology, Anthropology and
History of Peru, Lima

(Opposite, lower left) Phallic Fertility Object
Chucuito origin (Puno) (ca. A.D. 1400)
Height: 79 cm (31.2 in) Diameter: 31 cm (12.1 in)
National Museum of Archaeology, Anthropology and
History of Peru, Lima

Objects such as this, fastened to walls or placed in the middle of agricultural fields, were thought to promote fertility.

(Opposite, lower right) Pitcher Depicting Supernatural
Felines in the Shape of a Crescent Moon
Ceramic
Chancay (A.D. 1200–1450)
Height: 51 cm (19.9 in) Diameter: 39 cm (15.5 in)
National Museum of Archaeology, Anthropology and
History of Peru, Lima

(Left to right) Pitcher in the Form of a Corn Deity
Height: 22 cm (8.6 in) Diameter: 16 cm (6.3 in)

Pitcher in the Form of a Squash
Height: 16 cm (6.3 in) Diameter: 17 cm (6.7 in)

Pitcher in the Form of Cucumbers
Height: 19 cm (7.4 in) Diameter: 14 cm (5.5 in)

Pitcher Depicting Guanabana Fruit
Height: 20 cm (7.8 in) Diameter: 23 cm (9 in)
Chimú (A.D. 1100–1450)

Pitcher in the Form of a Peanut-Person
Height: 23 cm (9 in) Diameter: 16 cm (6.3 in)

Ceramic
Moche (A.D. 50–800)
National Museum of Archaeology, Anthropology and
History of Peru, Lima

*Effigies of edible food, like those depicted above, may have
been created to celebrate specific occasions, to use as offerings
to the gods, or to include in burials, ensuring nourishment for
the dead. Of particular interest here is the anthropomorphic
peanut on the far right, which reflects the Moche belief in
animism. Vegetables depicting faces also seem to have been
important. The peanut held an average status, which is why it
is often depicted with a human face. The potato, ranking much
lower, often appears with deformities, and corn, as shown on
the far right, usually takes the form of deity.*

people. Andean farmers still offer her a coca leaf,
chicha beer, and prayers on major agricultural
occasions.

The iconographic portrayal of supernatural beings
is abundant in ancient Peruvian art, and dates back
more than three thousand years. The image of a
conspicuously superior being is found in the initial
stages of high Andean civilization. The typical
Chavín image of a human with feline and raptorial-
bird attributes shows up periodically throughout
the various sequences of Andean culture. At
Chavín, such figures appear on the Raimondi Stela
and El Lanzón. This feline representation, in which
elements of human anatomy are sometimes
completely absent, may be the most ancient
representation known to us of an Andean god.
Supernatural beings of the highest level are found
in representations of the culture-hero gods Aiapaec
and Naymlap, and in those of Tiahuanaco and
Paracas-Nazca. All are anthropomorphic beings that
combine traits of both bird and feline; in this
context, they imply an evolutionary development of
the older winged feline of Chavín. In the archetypal
versions of Aiapaec, the figure bears wings. Feline
and ornithomorphic attributes are also evident in
the large figures at Tiahuanaco and Huari; from
their eyes fall large tears in the form of birds,

(Below, left to right) Pitcher Depicting a Ritual Race or Dance
Height: 28 cm (10.9 in) Diameter: 15 cm (5.9 in)

Pitcher Representing Warriors in Ritual Dance
Height: 29 cm (11.3 in) Diameter: 16 cm (6.3 in)

Ceramic
Moche (A.D. 50–800)
National Museum of Archaeology, Anthropology and History of Peru, Lima

(Below, right) Pitcher Representing the God Naymlap with his Children
Ceramic
Sicán (Lambayeque) (A.D. 700–1370)
Height: 21 cm (8.2 in) Diameter: 15 cm (5.9 in)
National Museum of Archaeology, Anthropology and History of Peru, Lima

Naymlap is the mythical founder of a pre-Chimú dynasty in Lambayeque, northern Peru. He is identified by a human face with bird characteristics like the hook nose shown here. From the eyes of Naymlap tears flow in the form of raindrops. The base of the pitcher has an incised stepped design depicting agricultural terraces and representing the abundance brought by Naymlap's tears.

(Above) Cup Depicting Water Symbols
Ceramic
Tiahuanaco-Huari (A.D. 800–1200)
Height: 9 cm (3.1 in) Diameter: 16 cm (6.2 in)
National Museum of Archaeology, Anthropology and History of Peru, Lima

Water symbols adorn this polychrome bowl; triangles ending in hooks represent waves, and the concentric circular designs depict rain drops.

(Above, left) Pitcher Depicting a Shaman Performing a
Rain Ceremony
Ceramic
Sicán (Lambayeque) (A.D. 700–1370)
Height: 24 cm (9.5 in) Diameter: 19 cm (7.5 in)
National Museum of Archaeology, Anthropology and
History of Peru, Lima

(Above, right) Pitcher Depicting Animals Running in a
Rain Storm
Ceramic
Chimú (A.D. 1100–1450)
Height: 24 cm (9.5 in) Diameter: 19 cm (7.5 in)
National Museum of Archaeology, Anthropology and
History of Peru, Lima

*Water is a fundamental resource depicted in many ancient
Peruvian artifacts. Within the circle of the monochrome
vessel above left is a shaman who performs rain promoting
rituals. Above the scene are iguanas with human faces. The
body of the adjacent vessel shows what appears to be foxes
running in rain. A stepped motif—a symbol of agricultural
terracing and an icon of the fertile earth—is discernable
near the spout.*

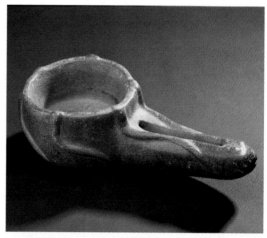

The Supernatural World

which have been interpreted as symbolic of the fertilizing rainwater of Pachamama.

Mythological literature indicates that those male beings who fertilize Mother Earth form the upper echelon in the hierarchy of the Andean pantheon. One of the most obvious expressions of the Andean gods' character as fertilizer-provider is the anthropomorphic wooden figure of the Huari, adorned with symbols referring to basic food products, found in the temples of Pachacamac near Lima. Images of connubial gods in which the male element radiates fertilizing solar rays are found especially in iconography derived from Huari, and in the valleys of Huara, Pativilca, and Casma on the Peruvian coast. Examples of Inca art that have survived seem to have votive content, and the feline and the falcon continue to occupy a place of honor among Inca iconographic elements, as may be seen in the heraldic shield of the Inca rulers drawn by Guamán Poma de Ayala.

(Top, right) Pitcher Depicting Women in Ritual Motion
Inca (A.D. 1200–1532)
Height: 77 cm (30.4 in) Diameter: 55 cm (21.5 in)
National Museum of Archaeology, Anthropology and History of Peru, Lima

(Right) Bowl Depicting a Supernatural Bird-Man
Ceramic
Nazca (A.D. 1–700)
Height: 47 cm (18.5 in) Diameter: 59 cm (23.3 in)
National Museum of Archaeology, Anthropology and History of Peru, Lima

(Opposite, center) Stone Phallic-Shaped Paccha
Basalt
Inca (A.D. 1200–1532)
Height: 9 cm (3.65 in) Diameter: 14 cm (5.5 in)
National Museum of Archaeology, Anthropology and History of Peru, Lima

The spout on this paccha, a pitcher used in fertility rituals, is in the shape of a phallus. Comprised of gray basalt, serpents are sculpted on the vessel's surface.

(Opposite, bottom) Ocarina made from an Incised Gourd
Ancón (A.D. 1200–1450)
Length: 7 cm (2.6 in) Diameter: 4 cm (1.4 in)
National Museum of Archaeology, Anthropology and History of Peru, Lima

This ocarina is a pyroengraved gourd with six openings.

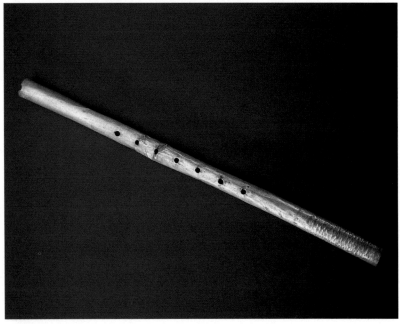

Through acts of worship, the sphere of the sacred could be manipulated to benefit mankind. The effectiveness of human intervention in the realm of supernatural powers depended on the intensity with which the rites were performed. Calamities that endangered the personal and collective welfare of ancient Peruvians were believed to have been caused by offenses to supernatural beings, and especially by a lack of intensity in worship. Offerings to the gods of sustenance and to other supernatural beings, including cruel human sacrifices, were considered essential to the efficacy of worship; in times of crisis, they were performed lavishly.

The diverse forms of worship in this region were due in part to the variety of divine or magical conditions that these people perceived. Such conditions were in general denoted by the term *huaca*, which can be translated as something holy. *Huaca* could refer to various unusual geographic features (including special stones, hills, lakes, and so on) heavenly bodies, atmospheric phenomena, mummies, amulets, idols, and even the Inca ruler himself in his capacity as a living god.

Communication with the supernatural world was achieved through *muchay*, worship or reverence. Muchay was performed by removing one's sandals, gesticulating, throwing kisses, murmuring supplications, bowing one's shoulders in humility, puffing out one's cheeks to blow in the direction of the object worshiped and so on. Other forms of

(Top left) Copper Musical Bells
Chimú (A.D. 1100–1450)
Height: 3 cm (1.2 in) Diameter: 4 cm (1.6 in)
National Museum of Archaeology, Anthropology and History of Peru, Lima

This copper rattle with sleigh-like bells was originally mounted on a staff.

(Left) Silver Flute
Chimú (A.D. 1100–1450)
Height: 48 cm (18.8 in) Diameter: 2 cm (.8 in)
National Museum of Archaeology, Anthropology and History of Peru, Lima

The Supernatural World

(Above) Whistling Pitcher Depicting a Seated Man
Ceramic
Moche (A.D. 50–800)
Height: 24 cm (9.5 in) Diameter: 17 cm (6.7 in)
National Museum of Archaeology, Anthropology and
History of Peru, Lima

*Musical instruments were common among the ancient
Peruvians. The figure shown above wears a loincloth or
huara, indicating that he is male.*

(Top right) Pitcher Representing a Man Playing a Pipe
Ceramic
Sicán (Lambayeque) (A.D. 700–1370)
Height: 21 cm (8.1 in) Diameter: 15 cm (5.8 in)
National Museum of Archaeology, Anthropology and
History of Peru, Lima

*This sculpted monochrome vessel depicts a seated man
with crossed legs playing a* quena, *or Peruvian flute.*

(Right) Pitcher Depicting a Man Playing a Drum
Ceramic
Chimú (A.D. 1100–1450)
Height: 14 cm (5.7 in) Diameter: 18 cm (7 in)
National Museum of Archaeology, Anthropology and
History of Peru, Lima

*This monochromatic sculpted vessel shows a simple
musical scene. The astonishing array of percussion and
wind instruments that have been excavated from Peruvian
burials reveals the importance of music in their lives.*

contact with supernatural beings were made through oracles who rendered predictions about important future events to shamans and priests.

To make an offering was an act of paying tribute. Offerings were both voluntary and compulsory. One widespread, popular offering was *mullo*, a powder made of ground seashells, which was linked to fertility through its association with water; another offering was coca, which would be chewed and then thrown into stone cairns, a ritual act called *Togana*. The mummified dead were offered special

(Top left) Double-Chambered Whistling Pitcher
Ceramic
Vicús (B.C. 200–A.D. 200)
Height: 17 cm (6.5 in) Diameter: 22 cm (8.6 in)
National Museum of Archaeology, Anthropology and History of Peru, Lima

Consistent with Vicús style, this piece is decorated with a darkened geometric design. On top of the front chamber is a roofed dwelling. The walls are painted with symbolic motifs, and inside is a man wearing a diadem and earrings.

(Center, left) Double-Chambered Whistling Pitcher
Ceramic
Vicús (B.C. 200–A.D. 200)
Height: 22 cm (8.6 in) Diameter: 30 cm (11.7 in)
National Museum of Archaeology, Anthropology and History of Peru, Lima

This whistling vessel is comprised of two chambers with a bridge handle and connecting clay tube. Atop the cubed chamber is a sculpted human figure blowing an antara, *or pan flute. A whistling mechanism was incorporated into the front chamber so that sounds could be made by blowing across the conical spout, or by manipulating the water within the vessel.*

(Left) Copper Flute
Chimú (A.D. 1100–1450)
Height: 3.12 cm (1.2 in)
National Museum of Archaeology, Anthropology and History of Peru, Lima

This copper object is in the form of a quena, *or flute, and has a sculptural mouthpiece and four finger holes.*

(Above, left to right) Double-Chambered Whistling Pitcher in the Form of Two Drums
Height: 26 cm (10.1 in) Diameter: 19 cm (7.4 in)

Pitcher in the Form of a Man Holding a Spondylus Shell
Height: 32 cm (12.5 in) Diameter: 20 cm (7.8 in)

Whistling Pitcher Representing a Human Figure Playing a Set of Pan Pipes
Height: 25 cm (9.8 in) Diameter: 21 cm (8.2 in)

Ceramic
Chancay (A.D. 1200–1450)
National Museum of Archaeology, Anthropology and History of Peru, Lima

The melodic whistling pitchers featured above depict musical themes. The spondylus shells decorating the central vessel were considered food for the gods by the ancient Peruvians. They were often set in jewelry or used for grave offerings.

(Below, left to right) Painted Ceramic Magic Tablets
Height: 20–22 cm (7.8–8.7 in) Width: 18–20 cm (7–7.8 in)

Chucu, Arequipa (13th century A.D.)
National Museum of Archaeology, Anthropology and History of Peru, Lima

Various symbols in the form of humans, animals, and raindrops adorn these ceramic-based tablets. They were recovered from an underground chamber, and may have been offerings to the gods in return for water and fertility.

jars containing grains, fruits, and liquids. Guinea pigs and llamas also served as important sacrificial offerings.

On occasion, the Inca did practice human sacrifice, sometimes involving young boys or girls. It appears that among the Inca the sacrifice of boys and girls was received as a form of tribute, called *capaccocha*, from the provinces. The person who was to serve as the *capaccocha* probably came to the capital city of Cuzco as an important person. One of the most frequent forms of sacrifice of such people seems to have occurred on mountain tops, probably in veneration of mountain gods. *Necropompa*, Spanish for death rite, was a special type of human sacrifice that consisted of immolations (voluntary or not) that were performed on the occasion of the death of an illustrious person. Human sacrifice, also performed to achieve greater agricultural fertility, may have drawn some of its rationale from an Andean belief that governed nature: death engenders life.

In addition to offerings, ancient Peruvians organized pilgrimages since at least the time of Chavín. One of the favorite *huacas*, or shrines, was the sanctuary of Pachacamac. Natural shrines such as those on the peaks of high mountains were also popular with pilgrims. The Collur Rit'i festival, a celebration that coincides with the Feast of Corpus Christi, follows ancient rites in which to this day people climb to heights of nearly 18,000 feet. Some of the pilgrims dress as bear men, imitating the gestures of animals and speaking in animal-like voices; they act as intermediaries between other pilgrims and supernatural beings. Originally, the Collur Rit'i was dedicated to water, and even today pilgrims return to their homes with pieces of ice carved from the mountain glaciers, symbolizing the fertility imparted by water.

(Opposite, top) Head of a Supernatural Being
Stone
Chavín de Huántar Replica (1000 B.C.–A.D. 200)
Height: 41 cm (16 in) Diameter: 39 cm (15.2 in)
National Museum of Archaeology, Anthropology and
History of Peru, Lima

*This stone head with hair made of serpents was one of a
series that depicted mystical transformations of men into
animals. The highland site of Chavín de Huántar was the
source of many of the religious motifs used for thousands of
years throughout Peru.*

(Opposite, bottom) Head of a Supernatural Being
Stone
Chavín de Huántar Replica (1000 B.C.–A.D. 200)
Height: 39 cm (15.2 in) Diameter: 47 cm (18.7 in)
National Museum of Archaeology, Anthropology and
History of Peru, Lima

*Dozens of heads, such as this one depicting a person in a
trance, were swept away by the alluvium that covered the
ruins in 1946.*

(Top right) Winged Fanged Deity
Stone
Chavín de Huántar Replica (1000 B.C.–A.D. 200)
Height: 49 cm (19.1 in) Width: 53 cm (20.7 in)
National Museum of Archaeology, Anthropology and
History of Peru, Lima

*An image of a supernatural bird with extended wings is
depicted on this ancient Peruvian stone. A feline mouth
with menacing fangs identifies the figure as a deity.*

(Right) The Supreme Deity
Stone
Chavín de Huántar Replica (1000 B.C.–A.D. 200)
Height: 53 cm (20.7 in) Width: 57 cm (22.6 in)
National Museum of Archaeology, Anthropology and
History of Peru, Lima

*This fanged deity carries spondylus and strombus shells,
which were believed to be symbols of the male and female
aspects of the universe. His hair is composed of serpents.*

Treasure

Little of the spectacular gold created by the Incas for their temples and palaces and for the ornamentation of their nobles exists today. Idols, adornments, and other precious objects were melted down in improvised furnaces by order of the Spanish, who amassed fabulous quantities of Inca gold, including the treasures gathered by Atahualpa as a ransom for his life.

Much of the existing gold objects from ancient Peru seen in the world's museums today date from pre-Inca times, and were looted, for the most part, from the tombs of the elite from cultures such as the Moche, Sicán (Lambayeque), Chimú, and Chavín. The north coast was the center of metallurgy in pre-Hispanic Peru. Gold was highly prized for its brilliance, malleability, and for the fact that it doesn't oxidize. It was considered a sacred metal that embodied the sun's creative energy and guaranteed survival, fertility, and abundance. Through artistic transformation, gold transcended its earthly source to become a tangible expression of status, power, and divinity.

(Above) This gold mask was found in the Moche tomb of the Old Lord of Sipán. In death, he took with him the treasures that signified power and influence during his life.

(Opposite) Gold Tumi with Inlaid Turquoise
Sicán (Lambayeque) (A.D. 700–1370)
Height: 25 cm (10 in)
National Museum of Archaeology, Anthropology and
History of Peru, Lima

A tumi is a ceremonial axe with a nonfunctional blade. This tumi represents the Sicán lord known as Naymlap. He is depicted with bird attributes such as wings and wing-shaped eyes. This piece is beautifully inset with turquoise, and has a particularly fine filigree base.

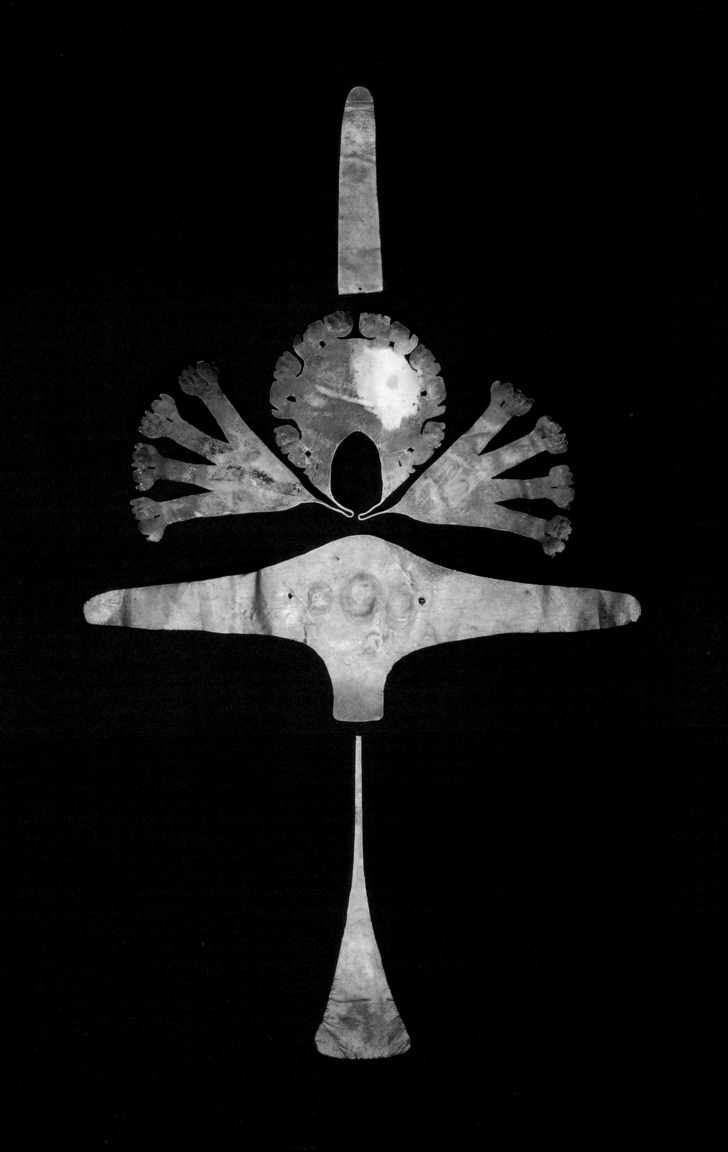

(Opposite, top to bottom) Gold Ornament in the Shape of
a Tongue
Height: 8 cm (3.1 in) Width: 1 cm (.4 in)

Gold Nose Ornament with Feline Whiskers
Height: 9 cm (3.4 in) Width: 19 cm (7.4 in)

Gold Headdress Ornament
Height: 24 cm (9.5 in) Length: 8 cm (3.1 in)

Gold Headdress Ornament in the Shape of a Feather
Height: 14 cm (5.6 in) Width: 4 cm (1.6 in)

Paracas (700 B.C.–A.D. 1)
National Museum of Archaeology, Anthropology and
History of Peru, Lima

*The gold tongue-shaped object at top has a perforation on
its upper extremity, which suggests it was probably displayed
hung. The laminated gold nose ornament below it features a
mustache-shaped design reminiscent of a feline. Similar
ornaments were commonly worn by the supernaturals
rendered in Nazca ceramics. Symbolic diadems such as the
one third from top are typically seen on figures in Paracas
and Nazca ceramics.*

(Above, left to right) Gold Figurine of a Man
Height: 6 cm (2.4 in) Width: 1 cm (.4 in)

Inca (A.D. 1200–1532)
National Museum of Archaeology, Anthropology and
History of Peru, Lima

Silver Figurine of a Woman and Child
Height: 6 cm (2.4 in) Width: 2 cm (.8 in)

Titicaca Basin (A.D. 1200–1532)
National Museum of Archaeology, Anthropology and
History of Peru, Lima

*The male figurine shown above left displays exaggerated
earlobe piercings. The anthropomorphic gold female statue
above right wears clothing that stretches down to her
ankles. In one hand she holds a baby, and in the other she
carries an* apacha, *or bag.*

During the Early Horizon, new metallurgy techniques were implemented and mastered, such as soldering, sweat welding, repoussé, and inlaying. Gold was used primarily for display in architectural settings, personal adornment, and ritual objects. The lavishness and abundance of gold pieces found in burials at Chavín present evidence of emerging social inequality during the Early Horizon. In Chavín, the creation of gold objects seems to have been stimulated in part by the spread of the Chavín cult, and the desire to convey the power of the cult through new, more extravagant technologies and techniques. While hammering was already widely used, sweat welding and soldering began in Chavín. Similar burial objects have been found in Kuntur Wasi, including crowns and ear ornaments that bear a style and religious symbolism related to Chavín.

Among the world's richest archaeological discoveries are the spectacular artifacts recovered from the tomb of the Old Lord of Sipán in 1989. Near his tomb, other elites were buried with the ornate gold, silver, and copper objects that affirmed their noble status. In one tomb, a warrior was found in full regalia with weaponry. Also discovered were images and implements related to a sacrifice ceremony. The Old Lord of Sipán was buried in a decorative headdress, with high-status earplugs, and an elaborate necklace of gold spiders set in a web-like

(Above) Gold Bowl with Designs of Faces in Relief
Chimú (A.D. 1100–1450)
Height: 7 cm (2.7 in) Width: 15 cm (5.9 in)
National Museum of Archaeology, Anthropology and History of Peru, Lima

Anthropomorphic heads with feline ears decorate this wide-based bowl.

(Opposite, top) Gold and Copper Repoussé Tunic for a Mummy
Chimú (A.D. 1100–1450)
Height: 37 cm (14.6 in) Width: 46 cm (18.1 in)
National Museum of Archaeology, Anthropology and History of Peru, Lima

Agricultural terraces, which make a cruciform shape when joined, comprise the principal motif on this repoussé breastplate.

(Opposite, bottom) Silver Crown with Cutwork Bird Designs
Chimú (A.D. 1100–1450)
Height: 3 cm (1.2 in) Diameter: 46 cm (18 in)
National Museum of Archaeology, Anthropology and History of Peru, Lima

The base of this silver crown features intricate cutwork of birds framed in squares.

(Opposite, left to right) Gold Figurine of a Woman
Height: 9 cm (3.5 in) Width: 2 cm (.8 in)

Silver Figurine of a Woman
Height: 6 cm (2.4 in) Width: 1 cm (.4 in)

Gold Figurine of a Woman
Height: 5 cm (2 in) Width: 1 cm (.4 in)

Gold Figurine of a Woman
Height: 6 cm (2.4 in) Width: 1 cm (.4 in)

Inca (A.D. 1200–1532)
National Museum of Archaeology, Anthropology and History of Peru,
Lima

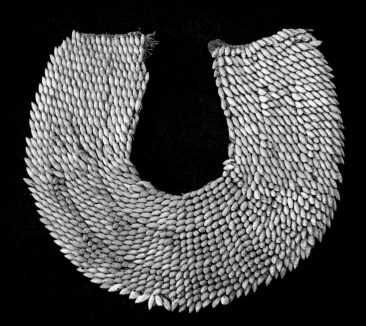

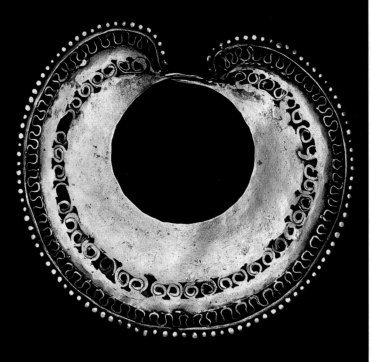

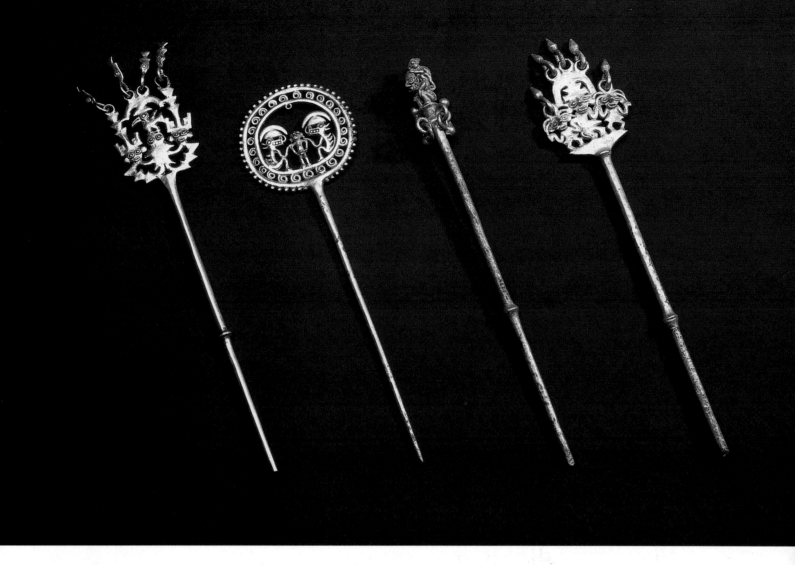

(Above) Silver and Gold Pins
Chimú (A.D. 1100–1450)
Length: 25 cm (10 in)
National Museum of Archaeology, Anthropology and History of
Peru, Lima

*These silver and gold decorative pins, featuring various human
and animal shapes, were used to fasten items of clothing.*

(Opposite, top left) Gold Diadem
Nazca (A.D. 1–700)
Height: 18 cm (7.1 in) Width: 24 cm (9.4 in)
National Museum of Archaeology, Anthropology and History of
Peru, Lima

(Opposite, top right) Bracelet of Hollow Gold Balls
Moche (A.D. 50–800)
Height: 3 cm (1.2 in) Width: 3 cm (1.2 in)
National Museum of Archaeology, Anthropology and History of
Peru, Lima

(Opposite, center left) Necklace with Eighteen Rows of Shells
Ancón (Date Unknown)
Height: 18 cm (7.1 in) Width: 24 cm (9.4 in)
National Museum of Archaeology, Anthropology and History of
Peru, Lima

(Opposite, center right) Gold Filigree Nose Ornament
Vicús (200 B.C.–A.D. 200)
Height: 5 cm (2 in) Width: 6 cm (2.4 in)
National Museum of Archaeology, Anthropology and History of
Peru, Lima

(Opposite, bottom left) Gold Ornament for a Pierced Lower Lip
Chimú (A.D. 1100–1450)
Height: 1 cm (.4 in) Width: 2 cm (.8 in)
National Museum of Archaeology, Anthropology and History of
Peru, Lima

(Opposite, bottom right) Gold Plume for a Headdress
Pukara or Tiahuanaco-Huari (200 B.C.–A.D. 800)
Height: 31 cm (12.1 in) Width: 5 cm (2 in)
National Museum of Archaeology, Anthropology and History of
Peru, Lima

*This stylized gold feather was part of an ancient Peruvian
headdress. In addition to various water symbols, it depicts an
embossed figure with a zoomorphic fanged face.*

(Above, left to right) Spondylus Shell Necklace
South Coast (Date Unknown)
Height: 61 cm (24 in)

Necklace of Silver Balls and Cones
Chimú (A.D. 1100–1450)
Height: 42 cm (16.4 in)

Gold, Silver, and Spondylus Shell Necklace
North Coast (Date Unknown)
Height: 47 cm (18.4 in)

Olivine and Gold Necklace
Moche (A.D. 50–800)
Height: 43 cm (16.8 in)

National Museum of Archaeology, Anthropology and
History of Peru, Lima

(Right) Copper Repoussé Tunic for a Mummy
Chimú (A.D. 1100–1450)
Height: 65 cm (25.4 in) Length: 62 cm (24.6 in)
National Museum of Archaeology, Anthropology and
History of Peru, Lima

*This copper pectoral is decorated with geometric shapes
and bird imagery, and has perforations that allowed it to be
attached to a tunic.*

Treasure

lattice. The necklace suggests that he may have played a primary role in the sacrifice ritual. The spiders symbolize the ceremony over which he presided, which involved the taking and consumption of blood.

In Inca society, gold was possessed only by the emperor and by nobility. A mark of status, it elevated the supreme leaders to the level of demigods, particularly since it was considered to have been bestowed by Inti, the Sun God. (An Inca creation myth declares that humanity had originated from three eggs, one of gold, one of silver, and another of copper. The first Inca rulers and their noble women came from the gold and silver eggs, and the common people came from the copper egg.)

Both silver and copper were regularly used by ancient metalworkers. Silver was sometimes seen as a symbol of the moon, and could be linked to the feminine, particularly to Pachamama, the Earth Goddess or Mother Earth. Adornments, royal table service, and idols were made from silver. Tools such as axes were made from copper, and bronze was used in the manufacture of weapons. These metals also appeared frequently in the form

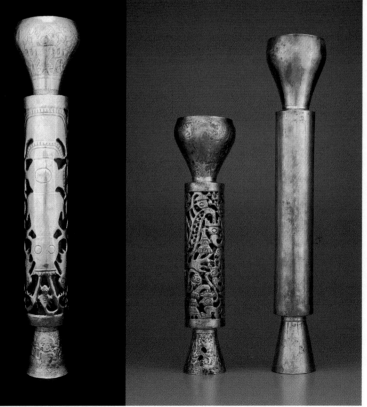

(Far left to right) Gold Ceremonial Cup
Height: 48 cm (8.8 in) Diameter: 11 cm (4.3 in)

Silver Ceremonial Cup
Height: 38 cm (14.9 in) Diameter: 8 cm (3.1 in)

Silver Ceremonial Cup
Height: 50 cm (19.5 in) Diameter: 9 cm (3.5 in)

Chimú (A.D. 1100–1450)
National Museum of Archaeology, Anthropology and History of Peru, Lima

These silver and gold ceremonial cups crown long handles that rest atop pedestals, which are also rattles.

(Above) Gold Repoussé Vase
Sicán (Lambayeque) (A.D. 700–1370)
Height: 21 cm (8.2 in) Diameter: 17 cm (6.7 in)
National Museum of Archaeology, Anthropology and History of Peru, Lima

This vase portrays the Sicán lord known as Naymlap.

of alloys, such as *tumbaga*, which was composed of gold and copper. Platinum was used infrequently, due to the difficulty of achieving its exceptionally high melting point. Ancient Andeans did, however, combine platinum grains with gold dust to form a molten mass that, after cooling, could be hammered and reheated, eventually becoming a workable material.

Metals were purified in various types of furnaces, such as, for example, the *huayra*, a small clay furnace perforated with small holes and activated by the wind. Huayras may have been used in creating the treasures of Atahualpa, the last Inca emperor.

(Above) Gold Ear Ornament
Sicán (Lambayeque) (A.D. 700–1370)
Height: 14 cm (5.5 in) Diameter: 13 cm (5.1 in)
National Museum of Archaeology, Anthropology and History of Peru, Lima

Large ear spools were a common form of personal adornment throughout the Americas. Some of the shafts reached diameters of more than one inch.

(Top left) Silver Cup in the Form of a Bird-Man
Chimú (A.D. 1100–1450)
Height: 16 cm (6.2 in) Diameter: 9 cm (3.5 in)
National Museum of Archaeology, Anthropology and History of Peru, Lima

The anthropomorphic design of this cup was created by hammering laminated plates over a wooden mold.

(Bottom left) Enameled Wooden Cup or Quero
Inca/Colonial (ca. late 1500s)
Height: 18 cm (7 in) Width: 15 cm (5.9 in)
National Museum of Archaeology, Anthropology and History of Peru, Lima

(Top right) Silver Repoussé Cup
Height: 24 cm (9.4 in) Diameter: 16 cm (6.2 in)

(Center right) Silver Bowl Depicting Frogs and Tadpoles
Height: 5 cm (2 in) Width: 14 cm (5.5 in)

Chimú (A.D. 1100–1450)
National Museum of Archaeology, Anthropology and History of Peru, Lima

A fishing scene is depicted on the silver repoussé cup at top right. Embossed images of frogs and toads adorn the double-bottomed bowl at center right.

(Bottom right) Incised Wooden Cup or Quero
Inca (A.D. 1200–1532)
Height: 11 cm (4.3 in) Width: 9 cm (3.5 in)
National Museum of Archaeology, Anthropology and History of the Peru, Lima

This wooden ceremonial cup, or quero, features flared walls with incised designs.

(Below) Gold Clasp with Textile Braids
Paracas (700 B.C.–A.D. 1)
Height: 5 cm (2 in) Width: 5 cm (2 in)
National Museum of Archaeology, Anthropology and History of Peru, Lima

This laminated gold object was hammered over a mold. It depicts a set of pincers, which may have been used to trim hair from a beard or mustache.

Suggested Reading

Alva, W. and C. B. Donnan. *Royal Tombs of Sipán.* Los Angeles: Fowler Museum of Cultural History, University of California, Los Angeles, 1993.

Anton, Ferdinand. *The Art of Ancient Peru.* New York: G. P. Putman's Sons, 1972.

Bankes, George. *Peru Before Pizarro.* Oxford: Oxford University Press. 1977.

Baudin, Louis. *Daily Life in Peru.* Translated by Winifred Bradford. New York: Macmillan, 1962.

Bauer, Brian S. *The Development of the Inca State.* Austin: University of Texas Press, 1992.

Bawden, Garth. *The Moche.* Cambridge: Blackwell Publishers Inc., 1996.

Beals, Carleton. *Nomads and Empire Builders.* Philadelphia: Chilton Company, Book Division, 1961.

Beltrán, Miriam. Cuzco: *Window on Peru* (2d Ed., Rev.). New York: Alfred A. Knopf, 1970.

Bennett, Wendell C. *Ancient Arts of the Andes.* Reprint. New York, Arno Press, 1966.

Bennett, Wendell C., and Janius B. Bird. *Andean Cultural History.* Garden City, NY: The Natural History Press, 1964.

Benson, Elizabeth P. *The Mochica: A Culture of Peru.* New York: Praeger, 1972.

Berrin, Kathleen, ed. *The Spirit of Ancient Peru: Treasures From the Museo Arqueológico Rafael Larco.* London: Thames and Hudson, Ltd., 1997.

Bingham, Hiram. *Lost City of the Incas: The Story of Machu Picchu and Its Builders.* New York Atheneum, 1971.

Bonavia, Duccio. *Mural Painting in Ancient Peru.* Translated by Patricia J. Lyon. Bloomington: University of Indiana Press, 1985.

Bruhn, Karen Olsen. *Ancient South America.* Cambridge: Cambridge University Press, 1994.

Burger, Richard L. *Chavin and the Origins of Andean Civilization.* London: Thames and Hudson Ltd., 1992.

Chang, K.C. *Art, Myth, and Ritual.* Cambridge: Harvard University Press, 1983.

Cobo, Bernabé. *History of the Inca Empire.* Edited and translated by Roland Hamilton. Austin: University of Texas Press, 1979.

_____. *Inca Religion and Customs.* Edited and translated by Roland Hamilton. Austin: University of Texas Press, 1990.

Cockburn, Aidan, and Eve Cockburn, Eds. *Mummies, Disease, and Ancient Cultures.* Abridged Ed. Cambridge: Cambridge University Press, 1980.

Collier, G. A., R. I. Rosaldo, and J. D. Wirth. *The Inca and Aztec States, 1400–1800: Anthropology and History.* New York: Academic Press, 1982.

D'Altroy, Terence N. *Provincial Power in the Inka Empire.* Washington D.C.: Smithsonian Institute Press, 1992.

D'Harcourt, Raoul. *Textiles of Ancient Peru and Their Techniques.* Translated by Sadie Brown. Seattle: University of Washington Press, 1975.

Donnan, Christopher B. *Ceramics of Ancient Peru.* Los Angeles: Fowler Museum of Cultural History, University of California, Los Angeles, 1992.

_____. *Moche Art of Peru.* Rev. Ed. Los Angeles: Museum of Cultural History, University of California, Los Angeles, 1978.

Garcilaso de la Vega, El Inca. [1609] *Royal Commentaries of the Incas and General History of Peru.* Translated by H. V. Livermore. Austin: University of Texas Press, 1987.

Guamán Poma de Ayala, Felipe. [1614] *Letter to a King: A Peruvian Chief's Account of Life Under the Incas and Under Spanish Rule.* New York: Dutton, 1978.

Hadingham, Evan. *Lines to the Mountain Gods: Nazca and the Mysteries of Peru.* New York: Random House. 1987.

Hass, Jonathan, Shelia Pozorski, and Thomas Pozorski, eds. *The Origins and Development of the Andean State.* Cambridge: Cambridge University Press,1987.

Hemming, John. *The Conquest of the Incas.* New York: Harcourt Brace Jovanovich, 1970.

_____. *The Incas and Their Ancestors.* New York: Harcourt Brace Jovanovich, 1989.

_____. *Monuments of the Incas.* Boston: Little, Brown and Company, 1982.

Hyslop, John. *Inca Settlement Planning.* Austin: University of Texas Press, 1990.

Kolata, Alen. *The Tiwanaku: Portrait of an Andean Civilization.* Cambridge: Blackwell Publishers Inc., 1993.

Keatinge, Richard W., Ed. *Peruvian Prehistory.* Cambridge: Cambridge University Press, 1988.

Kirkpatrick, Sidney D. *Lords of Sipán: A True Story of Pre-Inca Tombs, Archaeology, and Crime.* New York: William Morrow and Company, Inc., 1992.

Kosok, Paul. *Life, Land and Water in Ancient Peru.* New York: Long Island University Press, 1965.

Lanning, Edward P. *Peru Before the Incas.* Englewood Cliffs, N.J.: Prentice Hall, 1967.

Lehmann, Walter. *The Art of Old Peru.* New York: Hacker Art Books, 1975.

Lumbreras, Luis G. *The Peoples and Cultures of Ancient Peru.* Translated by Betty J. Meggers. Washington, D.C.: Smithsonian Institute Press, 1974.

Masuda, Shozo, Izumi Shimada and Craig Morris, Eds. *Andean Ecology and Civilization: An Interdisciplinary Perspective on Andean Ecological Complimentarity.* Tokyo: University of Tokyo Press, 1985.

Moseley, Michael. *The Incas and Their Ancestors.* London: Thames and Hudson, Ltd., 1992.

Moseley, Michael and Kent Day, Eds. *Chan Chan: Andean Desert City.* Albuquerque: University of New Mexico Press, 1982.

Paul, Anne, ed. *Paracas Art and Architecture: Objects and Context in South Coastal Peru.* Iowa City: University of Iowa Press, 1991.

Protzen, Jean-Pierre. *Inca Architecture and Construction at Ollantaytambo.* Oxford: Oxford University Press, 1993.

Richardson III, James B. *People of the Andes.* Washington D.C.: Smithsonian Institute Press, n.d.

Rick, John W. *Prehistoric Hunters of the High Andes.* New York: Academic Press, 1980.

Rowe, John H. *Chavín Art: An Inquiry into its Form and Meaning.* New York: The Museum of Primitive Art, 1962.

Silverman, Helaine. *Cahuachi in the Ancient Nasca World.* Iowa City: University of Iowa Press, 1993.

Silverblatt, Irene. *Moon, Sun, and Witches.* Princeton: Princeton University Press, 1987.

Shimada, Izumi. *Pampa Grande and the Mochica Culture.* Austin: University of Texas Press, 1994.

Stierlin, Henri. *Art of the Incas and Its Origins.* Translated by Betty Ross and Peter Ross. New York: Rizzoli, 1984.

Stone-Miller, Rebecca. *Art of the Andes from Chavín to Inca.* London: Thames and Hudson, Ltd., 1995.

Stone-Miller, Rebecca, ed. *To Weave for the Sun: Ancient Andean Textiles.* London: Thames and Hudson, Ltd., 1994.

Townsend, Richard F., Ed. *The Ancient Americas: Art from Sacred Landscapes.* Chicago: Prestel in association with The Art Institute of Chicago, 1992.

Acknowledgments

HB Hiram Bingham
JR John Rick
LM Loren McIntyre
NB Nathan Benn
PSR Philipp Scholz Rittermann
TG Todd Gipstein
WK Wolfgang Kaehler

All object photographs are by Philipp Scholz Rittermann unless otherwise noted.

Special thanks to John Rick, Department of Anthropology, Stanford University, for his generous assistance, and for providing access to his unique Stanford archive.

Thanks also to Marco DiPaul, National Geographic Society Image Collection.

Front Matter, pp. 1–23

Introduction, pp. 24–35

The Natural World, pp. 36–61

The Cultures of Ancient Peru, pp. 62–77

Empire of the Incas. pp. 78–91

Death and Burial, pp. 118–125

Treasure, pp. 144–157

Index